REINHARD
BONNKE

HELL EMPTY HEAVEN FULL

STIRRING COMPASSION FOR THE LOST

PART ONE

HELL EMPTY HEAVEN FULL

Part I

Stirring Compassion for the Lost

Reinhard Bonnke
with George Canty

So that by all possible means I might save some.
1 Corinthians 9:22

HELL EMPTY HEAVEN FULL
Part I
Stirring Compassion for the Lost

Reinhard Bonnke with George Canty
English

Copyright © E-R Productions LLC 2006
ISBN 1-933106-56-5

Edition 1, Printing 1
10,000 copies

Cover Design: Brand Navigation, U.S.A.
Typeset: Roland Senkel
Photographs by: Rob Birkbeck
Oleksandr Volyk
Robert Russell
Mark Theisinger
Roland Senkel

E-R Productions LLC
P.O. Box 593647
Orlando, Florida 32859
U.S.A.

www.e-r-productions.com

Printed in Singapore

Contents

Evangelism

There is but one God, the Father,
from whom all things came and for whom we live;
and there is but one Lord, Jesus Christ,
through whom all things came
and through whom we live.

1 Corinthians 8:6

Science and its marvels scan the heavens and give us access to the terrifying stretches of space and time. We can now look across the endless beyond, the velvety dark sky glittering with the gleam of uncountable galaxies. Our world survives in the midst of swirling infinities. We peer into the expanse above us and the sight swamps our minds and overwhelms our spirit.

Amid the wheeling galactic systems, the countless worlds like dust clouds and the whole engulfing vortex, do we have any significance? In this infinity can the weak voices of our proclamation of the cross register anything? What use is our gospel message against the vastness of such cosmic activity?

There is only one true answer: "These are the things of God." He is their explanation, full and adequate. Creation is the signature of the Almighty. He formed and cast all visible things for himself. He hammered them out on his anvil to fit himself. We are finitely little for these infinite splendors but God the Creator is too great for anything less. The glory of the heavens is only a pale reflection of his glory. The burning nebulae are jewels that fell from his garments and scattered as he passed by. The Milky Way is a ring for his little finger. *"By his breath the skies became fair and these are but the outer fringe of his works,"* says Job (26:13).

God created all things and told us why; he did not leave us guessing. His word is greater than Creation. He has left us here in his world with his word and for his word, creatures of understanding amid mindless dust clouds of swirling stars.

I saw an angel flying in mid-air,
and he had the eternal gospel to proclaim
to those who live on the earth
– to every nation, tribe,
language and people.

Revelation 14:6

Creation relates only to the Creator. Nothing exists for itself; no one exists in isolation from others – except rebellious sinners, who then lose their only validity, which is God. We are not our own meaning and without God we are irrelevant. Without God our world, its commerce, its industrious activities, its governments and its institutions become vanity and vexation of spirit, as motiveless as the wind that blows from south to north and back again (see Ecclesiastes 1:6).

You are worthy, our Lord and God,
to receive glory and honor and power;
for you created all things,
and by your will they were created
and have their being.

Revelation 4:11

The heavens declare God's glory and his word articulates it. That is the word we preach, the good news we share. There cannot be any other word; only one word can be true, just as existence can have only one reason and only one meaning. The unchangeable truth is that if the world does not relate to the gospel, it relates to nothing. If the world has nothing to do with the Church of Jesus Christ, it is nothing and going nowhere.

The gospel explains it all and nothing else does. Disown the gospel and darkness falls. No other voice tells us what the world is for; no other light illuminates the mystery of our own presence on earth.

Our message is far more than forgiveness and heaven. Our calling is to put a kind hand on the shoulder of the world and turn it round to see God. It will adore him. The Lord is the Savior. He is not there for us; we live for him. He saves us for himself, for his own glory. Our preaching does not end in people but in God. He takes delight in what he does for us. He loves because to love gives him joy. He loves beyond all the parameters of human affection and makes even the assault of the cross an expression of his love. His pain asserts it. He finds satisfaction in giving, pouring himself out to us, surrounding us with wonders, making his redeemed the garden of delight in which he walks.

To proclaim the gospel is to move for him, act with him, love in him, and delight in his joy as the privilege, meaning and purpose of all life. From the first to last chapter of this book we want to share our own inspiration with you, to galvanize his people to join in his work and to magnify his glorious name. God is the God of salvation. That is the ABC and the XYZ of our knowledge.

I desire to do your will, O my God;
your law is within my heart.
I proclaim righteousness in the great assembly;
I do not seal my lips, as you know, O Lord.
I do not hide your righteousness in my heart;
I speak of your faithfulness and salvation.
I do not conceal your love and your truth
from the great assembly.

Psalm 40:8-10

God has raised up the greatest gospel army ever seen. Such potential has never before been achieved in the whole history of the Church. It could be significant of the last days before Jesus comes. In the 21st century I picture us poised for take-off. It is not hard to visualize worldwide gospel impact once these huge battalions are mustered. The Church is the arm of God and the most effective force for good on earth.

These chapters aim to help mobilize the hosts of the Lord – a purpose they share with God's book, the Bible. Gospel proclamation is the finest adventure this life affords.

God offers us a partnership in his business and his business is salvation. This is not a book of dramatized illustrations or "anecdotal theology" but draws entirely on God's word to set us going as we seek to follow Jesus in his salvation purposes. Today's Christian literary fashion is about Christian living and Christian needs. These are not in dispute but the prior need is that of 4 billion lost souls. The word of God is there to help us to help them.

God has given us intelligence that we can use to find ways to implement his salvation purposes. We are gospel partners, entrepreneurs, agents of salvation, *"that by all possible means we might save some"* (1 Corinthians 9:22).

We must have resources, systems, plans, organization, and equipment. The danger is that we become more concerned with the machinery than the product. Machine-minding is necessary but only so that it continues to do its job. Organization never saves souls; only people can do that. Whatever plan we adopt, we still have to work at the "coal face" – and that means directly with people. Organization machinery will not do it for us.

Excitement about new approaches agitates the churches time after time. It raises hopes that if we do this or that, adopt the latest technique, follow the new formula, thousands will soon appear in church and revival will come. When someone is inspired with a new idea, it can be effective while he or she operates it. Others may adopt it, too, and it may do well because of the enthusiasm behind it. Our power in any scheme is only push power. We are the motor. God does not use methods; he uses people with methods, not casual labor. Success in genuine church growth, actual conversions, is 90 percent enthusiasm and 10 percent method.

Methods and systems transplanted from one part of the world to another have grown in different soil, against different cultural backgrounds. Knowing how to grow oranges in Florida will not be any use when trying to grow potatoes in Germany. No evangelistic scheme is universally applicable. To cultivate different gardens needs different methods because of different local conditions. The seed is always the same, but the ground is not.

It is absolutely vital to know God's word, the rock of Holy Scripture. It is the grindstone on which we sharpen our harvesting tools. Today is the time for bringing in the sheaves, for feasting, for setting the angels dancing in the brightness of God's joy.

Our vision is the divine aim to save the world. We set about fulfilling that vision by all the ways we can as God leads. Today the conversion figures run into tens of millions. Far more people are being born again than are actually being born. The man Christ Jesus is the colossus of modern times, bestriding the continents. He has no competitors. No man has had his following. In the words of an old hymn, "he plants his footsteps in the sea and rides upon the storm."

Communism tried to bury God, but God has buried communism. They patted down Christ's grave, but he was behind them, patting them on the shoulder. Christ's enemies are outnumbered, outclassed, outthought, and outlived by the millions that love him. A pop singer recently boasted that his band was more popular than Jesus Christ, but his claim has seemed rather hollow since the newspapers reported their break-up and their albums are rarely broadcast. The unknown man or woman who knows Christ lives on a higher level of life and is far more significant than any who do not know him, however rich or famous they might be.

Christians are being thrown into jail, tortured and murdered. Those who know Christ would rather suffer than be without him. Once you know Christ you cannot help but talk about him. The confessors and martyrs of Jesus are the true nobility of whom the world is not worthy. Saving our lost world is more important than the very stars the Creator made. Stars will grow dim, but *"those who are wise will shine like the stars for ever and ever"* (Daniel 12:3). *"The man who does the will of God lives for ever"* (1 John 2:17).

This world has false standards, false values, false gods, and false heroes. Its honor is a wreath of fading fame. True greatness is not bigness or spiritual prominence. It is doing God's will. To explain what that means and to provide encouragement to do likewise is what this book is for. It is "fresh bread," designed to impart new strength, energy and vigor, and its content is drawn from wide experience, thought, meditation, study, and Holy Spirit guidance.

The first book in the trilogy on evangelism, **Evangelism by Fire**, has been printed in some 50 languages and is in the hands of over 4 million readers. The second book is **Time is Running Out**, first published in 1999. These two books and two others – **Mighty Manifestations** and **Faith** – are essential reading on an online distance learning course. For several years we have been working on an immense project, the **Full Flame Films** series. This third exposition of evangelism has been written especially in connection with that project. All our books and films have the same objective – to inspire believers worldwide to be effective witnesses for Christ.

We have one lifetime only to reach our own generation. Each believer reaching others is the secret of expansion and always has been, *"that by all possible means we might save some."*

Evangelist Reinhard Bonnke
Author

Part 1

Now get up and stand on your feet.
I have appeared to you to appoint you as a servant and as a
witness of what you have seen of me and what I will show you.
I will rescue you from your own people and from the Gentiles.
I am sending you to them to open their eyes and to turn
them from darkness to light, and from the power of Satan
to God, so that they may receive forgiveness of sins and
a place among those who are sanctified by faith in me.

Acts 26:16-18

CHAPTER 1

Missing from Exodus

"Let my people go!"
Exodus 5:1

I had been reading the first book in the Bible, Genesis. As I moved on into the next book, Exodus, I noticed that something familiar was missing. Genesis speaks of the God of Creation, and I fully expected the Creator theme to continue in Exodus, but it didn't. Why?

Actually, I soon grasped why, as I will tell you shortly, but the first lesson in truth is that God is not just the Creator. His universe itself tells us a tremendous amount about him, but creating the universe is not the only thing he has done. Reading on, I soon reached Exodus 3, an extremely important chapter. There we see Moses standing before God and receiving secrets, wonderful things that had remained hidden since the dawn of mankind, things about God himself.

Receiving Secrets

Obviously we can know nothing about God unless he tells us; trying to work out his identity by applying human powers of reason or by guesswork is no better than lighting a match in the dark. God is light, so it is no use looking for him in the dark. *"The light shines in the darkness, but the darkness has not understood it"* (John 1:5). Seeking God by using human wisdom is like looking for the sun with a candle.

In fact, that is the very reason why I am writing this book: I want everyone to know the Lord and the part each of us plays in his overall design. Six times in Exodus he promises "You shall know that I am the Lord." In Ezekiel the same promise is made 43 times and in that one book there are over 70 references to knowing the Lord. What is more, Exodus shows us that the Lord also intended his enemies (the Egyptians) to know who he was! The evidence would seem to suggest that he does want people to know him!

Abraham knew God, even as a friend whom he could really trust. He called him the Almighty, or Most High God, but he did not know who or what he really was. Abraham, Isaac and Jacob never knew God like Moses did. They did not know God's name, which is most important.

First of all we need to realize that "god" is not a name, but a common noun used for a particular category of beings. *"There are many 'gods' and many 'lords'"* (1 Corinthians 8:5). When the apostle Paul visited Athens in AD 51, he discovered a shrine to an "unknown god" – nameless, without an identity. A long time before that, some 4,000 years ago, God was identified only by association with Abraham, as Abraham's God, and then as Isaac's and Jacob's God. After landing in trouble, Jacob told God that if he stayed with him on his journey, he would choose him as his God. A bargain, very patronizing! Yet God understood. Jacob's thinking was not very theological! He thought of God as the family God, a tribal deity, much as pagans think of their gods, but he was the "most high" of them all.

It is astounding that God allowed this liberty. People judged what God was by what Abraham did and the patriarch's actions did not always reflect God. People are said to be known by the company they keep, and if God keeps company with us, what do people think of him? What do people think about our God, our Lord Jesus, when they see us?

Abraham's grandson, Jacob, wanted to know God's name – who he really was. Plenty of gods had names. Jacob's wife Rachel had a bag full of them, images that she carried around in her saddle bag!

Then one night as he was traveling across the wilderness, sleeping with a stone for a pillow, in the quiet darkness Jacob had an encounter with a mysterious being. Jacob said, *"Please tell me your name!"* The only reply he was given was *"Why do you ask?"* (Genesis 32:29). God's name was still secret.

In Exodus, 400 years later, the theme is taken up again and the mystery solved. God reveals himself to Moses as fire, showing his temperament: *"God is a consuming fire"* (Hebrew 12:29). Moses saw the divine flame burning in a bush. God gave himself a personal name, distinguishing him from all other gods.

He said, *"I appeared to Abraham, to Isaac and to Jacob as God Almighty, but by my name YHWH I did not make myself known to them"* (Exodus 6:3). English Bibles usually translate the Hebrew word YHWH (read as Yahweh [Yahveh] or Jehovah) as LORD, printed in capital letters.

That is God's personal name, identifying him as the living, acting, and speaking Deity. Once he had made his name known, he acted on it. God demonstrates what he is. He confirmed with deeds what he had previously revealed in visions, dreams or words in the mind. No other "god" actually performs deeds.

Now what about the concept in Genesis that I missed in Exodus? When God spoke to Moses, he said nothing about being the Creator. People naturally think of God as the Creator. When I stopped to think about it, it seemed strange to me that he did not introduce himself to Moses as the God who was already known. The reason is that there are many sides to God, and through the years he has progressively taught mankind what he is in one lesson after another. His first lesson began with Moses, and we are in a highly privileged position today; many centuries later, so many things about God have already become known. Moses learned some fundamental facts about God. God told him, *"I have come down to rescue them* [my people] *from the hand of the Egyptians"* (Exodus 3:8).

God was showing himself in a new light, as more than a deliverer. He did not deliver only when asked. In Egypt, Israel had not asked to be delivered. They worshipped other gods and had no escape plans. Even Moses had no stomach for the venture; the people were not particularly cooperative, and Pharaoh was anything but willing to agree to the people leaving, but God delivered Israel by his own will, for his own honor and name. It was a demonstration for all time that he is a savior, a God who hates oppression, a living God who wants to save us.

God's business is with people, not planets or suns. Sooner or later we all realize that we need help, saving help. If we have only other people to help us, then we would despair. We need other people, but there are things that others cannot do. Jesus saves; no one else can do that.

What is Salvation?

In the Old Testament God made a covenant with his chosen people that he would be with them in everything they did, a promise that he has never withdrawn. Early Israel had little idea of heaven or of sin, either – something they had in common with the modern world. Salvation meant deliverance from sickness, enemies, plagues and droughts, the promise of God's blessing on the work of their hands, in their homes and on their families.

The Christian covenant is the forgiveness of sins and the promise of a future with God – a spiritual covenant. But God's first salvation promises have not been cancelled out. The apostle Paul wrote to the Corinthians, who had only the Old Testament to go by (the New Testament had not yet been compiled), to tell them, *"No matter how many promises God has made, they are 'Yes' in Christ"* (2 Corinthians 1:20). God cares about people and their daily lives; he always did and always will. Because he cares, he saves people from a hopeless destiny, forgiving sin and inviting sinners to walk with him.

The very word "save" in Bible Greek also means "heal." The covenant of God is both physical and spiritual, and that is the core revelation of the Charismatic revival. Pentecost is a physical-spiritual experience. It enhances every

> The Christian covenant is the forgiveness of sins and the promise of a future with God – a spiritual covenant.

doctrine in the book, and embraces every human need in body, soul and mind. God is not a lover of souls only, but of living people. As much as he hated Israel's bondage to slavery, he hates the bondage of everyone anyone who is in the grip of the devil and sin in any form.

God is like that; he always was like that and always will be. When Adam and Eve had sinned, their plight drew God to them, not merely to help them but to deal with what they brought down on the world, like opening Pandora's Box. The Lord went looking for them; *"Adam, where are you?"* he called (Genesis 3:9). Adam and his wife were naked and shivering, desperately trying to hide in shame. He restored and rehabilitated them and his promise to them encompassed the physical and the spiritual.

Sinners cannot save sinners. We are all trapped at the bottom of the pit and none of us can pull others out. Technology cannot touch the need of the human heart. Only the Almighty himself can reach out to us and fulfill our greatest longings. He cannot delegate the task to anyone else, not even to Michael, Gabriel, or the greatest angel in heaven. Human bondage is his problem alone. God said, *"I, even I, am the* LORD *and apart from me there is no Savior"* (Isaiah 43:11).

Only God can save, but he never does the work alone. He chose Moses to work with him in the tremendous undertaking to set Israel free. As we read on in the Bible, we see that pattern repeated time and again, God choosing people to work with him to bring about his purposes. That is what this book is about, the partnership of God and man with the objective of world deliverance;

the Lord beckons us to join him. He spun worlds, stars and galaxies out of his almighty hand without our aid, but commissioned Moses: *"Go and deliver my people!"* We not only work with one another, but work together with him.

Moses was not a mere observer but a participator operating in the might of Jehovah.

The LORD is my rock, my fortress and my deliverer;
my God is my rock, in whom I take refuge.
He is my shield and the horn of my salvation, my stronghold.
I call to the Lord who is worthy of praise
and I am saved from my enemies.

Psalm 18:2-3

Moses had become a retiring 80-year-old living quietly as a shepherd, but God dug him out of his comfortable life to take part in the greatest of all adventures, to shake Egypt. Moses began a new career of daring and energy. To go along with God is not a Sunday afternoon pastime. Serving God makes us partners with him in the one thing the whole Bible is about – deliverance! Jesus said, *"My Father is always at his work to this very day and I, too, am working"* (John 5:17).

If we want to know the Lord, we had better know who we are dealing with. When Christ called fishermen to follow him, they could never have guessed where he would lead. They learned by spending time with him, and then he sent them off to the ends of the earth. Learning from God is always a work experience. We learn that he is a Spirit who burns against anything that is opposed to his redeeming the lost. Our relationship is not about Hollywood emotions; it is a working partnership with a deliverer.

God appeared to Moses in living flames – but not just to give Moses an exciting experience. Christianity is not just religious feelings; that is one of today's gross heresies, making all religions equal provided that they arouse religious feelings. The Lord had desperately urgent business. It was so vital to him that he did more than send Moses into action; he sent his Son, sent his Holy Spirit, and ultimately sends us.

At the time of Moses every nation on earth depended on slave labor. However, regardless of the policies or economies pursued by nations, the Lord is a deliverer. He created the first free nation, stripping Egypt of gangs of forced labor. Slaves worked 7 days a week, but the Lord had different rules: *"Six days you shall labor and do all your work"* (Exodus 20:10). His people were not to be sweated labor, working like horses. He forbade even his priests to smell of sweat when at the altar.

We are working with God to set people free. The French philosopher Rousseau created a Communist slogan: "Man is born free but is everywhere in chains." The teachings that advocated submitting the individual will to the general

> As soon as we take an interest in evangelism, God takes an interest in us.

al will were a miserable failure. They led to political slavery, not freedom. People have many hang-ups and bondages; these include weakness, sinfulness, self-indulgence, guilt, unbelief, fear, and uncertainty. They keep psychologists, counselors and therapists busy, not to mention various religious sects. We need to go to the root of the matter. There is only one source of personal bondage: sin; and only one Savior from sin: Jesus.

The harsh truth about us all is our handicap of sin. God is concerned about that. Governments and their laws can penalize human failure, but cannot cure the cause. Jesus alone touches the deep springs of our personality. No one else has ever said, *"Son, your sins are forgiven. Get up, take your mat and walk"* (Mark 2:9). Nor has anyone else ever said, *"Go into all the world and preach the good news. Whoever believes and is baptized will be saved"* (Mark 16:16). There is no other good news than the gospel of salvation.

God's identity is encapsulated in the words of Isaiah 43:3: *"I am the LORD, your God, the Holy One of Israel, your Savior."* Similar words are used to introduce our Lord Jesus: *"You are to give him the name Jesus, because he will save his people from their sins"* (Matthew 1:21). Jesus is called "Savior" a score of times in the New Testament, and on every page he is shown to be our conquering Lord. The hand of power that molded the mountains is now stretched out to save.

As soon as we take an interest in evangelism, God takes an interest in us. We become people after his own heart. There is more to God than making mountains and stars, although he has done that, too. His priority is people. He runs the whole universe with a saving objective. Our troubles trouble him and he calls us to share his concern. That is our Great Commission, and the following chapters are meant to inspire and encourage you to be part of the greatest thing going on today in heaven and on earth.

Questions

Now that you have read this chapter, think of the answers to these questions. It will help to put some important truths into your spirit.

1. The God of Abraham became the God of Moses.
   What was the difference?
2. God made the world without help, but for salvation he seeks our help. How can you help?
3. Jesus saves spiritually and physically.
   What Bible evidence can you think of for that?

CHAPTER 2

Jesus out of Bounds

"We must do the work of him who sent me."

John 9:4

Jesus went to see a woman – and what a woman! The story is found in John 4.

An idyllic day. Warm sunshine. A young eastern woman in colorful clothing and carrying a pitcher on her shoulder approaches the well. A well nearer her home would have saved her a dusty walk, but gossiping women there would have involved her in an argument she preferred to avoid.

Men did not usually go to wells to draw water, but today a man was there, sitting quietly in the shade. Interesting ... but he was wearing Judean clothes. The woman hesitated. A man, yes ... but a Jew? Adjusting her veil, she studied him from a distance. Why was he there? If he really came from Judea, he must have been walking for a day or two.

She would wait till he left. No ... he was looking at her and then – a real "no-no" – he called over to her! A man, a Jew, calling to a Samaritan woman. What did he want? He smiled at her. Reassured, she turned boldly towards him.

"Will you give me a drink?" he asked. She stared at him. Give him a drink? Travelers always had a leather cup attached to their belt, but she noticed that he did not have one. Was he to use her cup? As she weighed him up, he seemed harmless enough and had a lovely voice. Venturing a step or two nearer, she put her water jar down, set her hands on her hips, and asked with a coquettish shrug, "You, a Jew, talking to me? What are you after?"

That was a moment that changed the world, although she was totally unaware of it. This was Jesus of Galilee wielding a sledge-hammer against the ancient wall of hatred between Jew and Gen-tile. She was astonished, too astonished to give him the drink. He broke in on her thoughts, *"If you knew the gift of God and who I am, you would have asked me for a drink and I would have given you living water."*

What was he talking about? He give her a drink? How was he going to do that when he did not even have a cup, let alone a water jar? She glanced over at the well, the only water in sight. Was he quite right in the head? He seemed rather charming, not like any Jew she had ever met before, but his religion and hers was differ-ent, especially when it came to matters concerning the well. Jacob had given them the well, and drinking from it was a religious sac-rament to Samaritans.

That woman went to the well every day. Jesus knew that. He also knew that the well water did not quench the thirst in her soul. No drink ever did, for anybody. Neither holy water nor sexual adventures could satisfy her. He made her an offer: *"The water I give you will become in you a spring of water welling up to eternal life."*

The man talked in riddles. Living water from a well? There was no such thing. Well water seeped in through underground chan-nels. Living water was an open stream coming from the hills, bub-bling and sparkling. She tried to humor him. *"So, you are greater than our father Jacob then, are you? Greater than Jacob who gave us this well? All right then, give me a drink of your living water! It will save me coming here every day."* Jesus smiled, and she saw him studying her, but where was his promised water? Instead, he said, *"Go and fetch your husband!"* With an arch look she said, *"Hus-band? I have no husband!"* His reply made the world spin round her: *"I know you haven't. But you have had five husbands, and the man you are living with now is not your husband."*

The arrow penetrated her conscience. She stared at him in amazement. How did he know about her? This odd man must be a prophet. What was she to say to a man like that? She was no thinker to argue and debate with him as other people did. Then it came to her: There was the perpetual bone of contention about Samaritans worshipping at Gerizim and Jews at Jerusalem. She was a Samaritan and he was a Jew, so which was right? It was a ready-made defense against the sharp perceptions of this stranger.

Human nature never changes. The woman's sisters and brothers are still around today, full of criticism, falling back on any old query to fend off spiritual realities and dodge the real issue. What she talked about – which religion is right – still provides an evasion and excuse today. On the surface, the question may seem legitimate. However, nobody really wants an answer. People could care less which the true religion is, or even if there is a true one. They bring it up because it deflects the challenge of the fact of Christ and turns faith into controversy.

Jesus knew what was in her and went straight for her soul. Faith is not a talking point but a life-issue. The man who treats it as problematic proves nothing; he merely reveals his character. The world invents conundrums to gag Christians. They treat us like dartboards on which to score points. However, this woman had to deal with Jesus himself, not religion. Jesus is still the question, and he says, "Give me your heart, not your opinions." He still confronts us today with a fact beyond debate. He is the truth; he cannot be a controversy. We cannot judge truth; it judges us.

Jesus' answer cut the ground from under the Samaritan's feet. True worshippers, he said, need neither Jerusalem nor Gerizim. God has no shrine. That is religion. He is with the true in spirit. Before King Solomon ordered all worship to be at Jerusalem, worshippers built altars wherever they lived. They had to travel to worship. Today the Lord's promise is never to leave us alone. There is no airport with direct flights to him. He is not a life's journey away. He is not a destiny, a Holy Grail or a future goal. He is the now-God. In fact, we cannot get away from him. The only choice we have is whether to turn our backs on him or face him. One way is completely dark. The other way is all light.

Moses told Israel long before, *"It is not up in heaven or beyond the sea. The word is very near you; it is in your mouth and in your heart"* (Deuteronomy 30:13-14). There is nowhere where worship is wrong. There is no wrong place and no wrong time; only people can be wrong, doing things in the wrong spirit. The apostolic word is *"I want men everywhere to lift up holy hands in prayer, without anger or disputing"* (1 Timothy 2:8). Ezekiel had prophesied to the Samaritan ancestors and gave God a name that tells us much the same thing: "Jehovah Shammah," "the LORD is there." God is not waiting for the church service to start. He is where we are. We only have to wake up to that fact.

> Jesus still confronts us today with a fact beyond debate. He is the truth; he cannot be a controversy. We cannot judge truth; it judges us.

God is always where we are

If there were places where God is not present, we could never find them, because as soon as we got there, he would be there: *"If I rise on the wings of the dawn, if I settle on the far side of the sea, even there your hand will guide me, your right hand will hold me fast"* (Psalm 139:9-10). God does not let us out of his sight and does not want us out of his sight. His love for us is vividly portrayed in Jesus' description of the Prodigal Son's return: The father ran up the road to meet him. When we knock on our heavenly Father's door, God himself opens it. The Lord is always where we are. Many people seem to think that God hovers about like an ambience in designated places, in churches, at holy sites, shrines and wells, in sacred ruins and cathedrals. That is a pre-Christian superstition.

Revivalist language can be bad theology. It often suggests that God visits certain places at certain times and is more present here than there, exerting greater energy in one place than another – God at his best! It befogs the view of God in Scripture. The Bible God is always at his best and is never low key, keeping something back. He has no sentimental attachment to favorite spots: *"The disciples went out and preached everywhere, and the Lord worked with them"* (Mark 16:20). Jesus said, *"Surely I am with you always, to the very end of the age"* (Matthew 28:20).

One French translation of Psalm 111:3 says, *"He is always faithful to himself."* [1] God is fully God, everywhere and always. His glory breaks through wherever circumstances provide the opportunity. His purposes and promises are constant, unaffected by time or place, never sporadic, never fickle. He has no off days or extra-busy days. His activities change, but he does not. His desire for the greatest good sees him take action to deal with conditions and circumstances.

The Samaritan woman knew no theology, so her next ploy was to challenge him to do what he said, give her living water. He did, although we do not know how or when. Whoever asks receives. The woman went through no dark night of the soul, no agony of conscience, no tears, no hysterics, no sinner's prayer, or any prayer at all, never expressed repentance and no supernatural manifestation was evident, but Jesus saved her. Somewhere along the road, going to the town or coming back, she received eternal life as unobtrusively as grass growing, drinking from the deep well of the mercy of God.

Jesus saves, even though the moment of salvation is not always glaringly obvious. Around the time that these very words were being written, well over one million precious Nigerians were meeting Jesus to experience salvation in one of our 5-day campaign

---

[1] « Il est pour toujours fidèle à lui-même. » (La Bible en français courant)

meetings. Tropical rain drenched them like a bathroom shower for hour after hour but it did not dampen their joy or deter them. They all testified to Christ and gave their names and addresses.

Emotionalism vs. the Emotion of the Gospel

The Samaritan woman had known many men, but meeting Jesus filled her soul. Strange reactions electrified her. She ran about the town's market place talking of a man but not about any of the 6 men she had known intimately in her life. Excited, she urged everyone, *"Come, see a man!"* Some surely thought, "What another man? She and her men!" Yet she convinced every man within reach of the need to go and see Jesus for themselves. She made it their hour of visitation, a historic privilege.

Jesus saved that woman in those odd circumstances and she was not even a seeking soul. He finds people who are not seeking. Take the gospel to anyone and it convinces them they have always needed it. Even if they have never heard of Christ, they need him and know it when the gospel reaches them. The gospel is not a general message shouted around for anybody who might be interested or is religiously inclined. The Bible is for people who have no faith, to give them faith. Fifty years ago nobody wanted a mobile phone. Now everyone feels they need one. Preaching Christ creates the market for salvation, and Jesus saves *"completely"* (Hebrew 7:25). Christ follows no saving formula or doctrine. He does not need a special atmosphere or religious surroundings. Some testify that they heard the gospel, made no decision, but felt clean and different, free from chaining habit. Pre-evangelism is not a prerequisite. The gospel creates its own success and its own atmosphere. We must distinguish between emotionalism and the emotion of the gospel. We can work people up, but the gospel works **in** people. The word rouses us to joy and exuberant worship. Jesus saves without a song and a dance but gives us a song and dance. Christian life may look tame, but then so does an electric cable till you touch it.

Jesus did not turn this woman into a religious freak. Christ just told her to bring her "husband" and off she went. If she brought her partner we don't know, but she exceeded her quota and brought everyone else's husband. What she did made her – a woman and a once sex-obsessed one at that – the world's first evangelist! The only message she had was Jesus. She could not debate about God; she knew nothing about him. Debate is not our commission. We are not religion pushers, church publicists or spiritual insurance salesmen. Evangelism is not the hard sell but simply the good news of Jesus Christ carried by a heart and mind enthusing about him.

Fire was lit in the woman's soul. That same fire took hold of the apostles. They lit the dark world like flaming torches, ablaze with the love of Jesus. *"To you who believe, he is precious,"* wrote Peter (1 Peter 2:7). Christ died, rose and ascended to heaven and the disciples proclaimed him. At the beginning, the highest authorities bombarded them with threats about what would happen if they ever mentioned Jesus' name again, driving their message home with a humiliating whipping. The next morning the disciples were preaching Jesus right under the noses of the authorities and *"day after day, in the temple courts and from house to house, they never stopped teaching and proclaiming the good news that Jesus is the Christ"* (Acts 5:42). Preaching the good news took priority over any threats and was expressed by the apostle Paul: *"Woe to me if I do not preach the gospel"* (1 Corinthians 9:16). That life aim is life.

Under Authority

The story in John's Gospel begins like this: *"Now he* [Jesus] *had to go through Samaria"* (John 4:4). Jewish travelers bypassed Samaritan country if they could, unless money and business were their reasons for going there, but for Jesus it was a case of "having to go" to Samaria. And he was not going there for money.

"Have to" in the Gospels (Greek *deo*) invariably implies an inner urgency, a personal compunction. Jesus came to Jacob's well doing the will of God, knowing it was the right time and place for him, as always; wherever Jesus went, his movements were never left to chance. He relaxed quietly at the well, alone where God wanted him to be. A few minutes later his disciples joined him with food and were shocked to find him in close public contact with a woman. They did not dare to say anything; they offered him some of the food that, after all, he had told them to go and buy. Food? Jesus' mind was on other things: *"My food is to do the will of him who sent me and to finish his work"* (John 4:34).

Four times in John's Gospel we read that Jesus was moved by the same imperative. Twice he said, *"The Son of Man must be lifted up"* (John 3:14, 12:34). He was absolutely clear about his purpose in life: *"I must do the work of him who sent me,"* he said (John 9:4) and *"I have other sheep. I must bring them also"* (John 10:16).

Luke's Gospel has more examples of what compelled Jesus: *"I must be about my Father's business"; "I must preach the good news of the kingdom of God"* (Luke 2:49 NKJV, 4:43). Jesus was under no illusions about what it would cost him; twice he said, *"The Son of man must suffer many things"* (Luke 9:22, 17:25). *"I must keep going today and tomorrow and the next day – for surely no prophet can die outside Jerusalem,"* he said (Luke 13:33). He reminded his listeners of what the prophets had foretold: *"Did not the Christ have to suffer these things?"* (Luke 24:26). The same Greek word is used in each of those verses. In every instance this "must" is related to salvation.

A Roman centurion asked Jesus to restore his paralyzed servant: *"Just say the word, and my servant will be healed"* (Matthew 8:8). Jesus was astonished at his faith but the centurion explained, *"I myself am a man under authority, with soldiers under me. I tell this one, 'Go', and he goes."* The centurion had authority because he was under authority. He could command because he obeyed commands. That Roman soldier had more than faith; he had perception and saw that Jesus also acted *"under authority"* to God. That meant that he had authority to command sickness to go and it would go.

Whatever Jesus did was "under authority." He had to do the will of his Father. Our salvation depended on it. His saving work was no casual operation or sideshow. For that matter neither was Creation, although God brought it into being simply by saying: *"Let there be light"* (Genesis 1:3). Salvation is, however, a far different matter. When Jesus told Mary and Joseph, *"I must be about my Father's business"* (Luke 2:49 NKJV), he was talking about the business of salvation. It was the Father's business for the Son to be born and for salvation to be his immediate and direct business. He came to earth to be our Savior. He was the Word that **spoke** at Creation, but for salvation the Word **came**. His coming was life-long, a sustained sacrifice climaxing in the most horrible death. That was love in its most ultimate form.

> Debate is not our commission. We are not religion pushers. Evangelism is the good news of Jesus Christ carried by a heart and mind enthusing about him.

Salvation was Jesus' great imperative. Our imperative is found in Mark 13:10: *"The gospel must first be preached to all nations."* Preaching does not happen all by itself; someone has to do it. Disciples and servants of Christ Jesus must be sent and must go. It is our Galilean call and our Macedonian call. Salvation could only be achieved by Christ's obedience to the Father and needs our obedience to Christ's command: *"Go into all the world and preach the good news ..."* (Mark 16:15).

Think about it!

Questions

1. Give 3 reasons why Jesus should not have spoken to the woman at the well and three reasons why he did.
2. What message made this non-Jew the world's first evangelist?
3. Why did Jesus have to go through Samaria?

*We no longer believe just because of what you said;
now we have heard for ourselves, and we know
that this man really is the Savior of the world.*

John 4:42

CHAPTER 3

Always Tomorrow

"Now is the day of salvation."
2 Corinthians 6:2

The best way to learn about evangelism is to look at how the greatest evangelist who ever lived did it.

Jesus befriended the woman of Samaria and showed her salvation, and then the disciples turned up. He made the occasion an opportunity to talk about evangelism and laborers in the harvest fields. Obviously what he had to say is of key importance for all who labor for Christ Jesus.

He had asked the woman to go home and fetch her husband. She had left him and now he saw her returning. He told the disciples to look, exclaiming, *"Open your eyes!"* What they saw astonished them. It was quite hilarious. The woman was leading a crowd of men. Normally, not a man in the town would have been seen talking to her. She had gone for her husband, and her excitement about a stranger at the well made every woman's husband in town ready to go with her.

That was the disciples' second surprise. The first had been when they found Jesus talking to a woman, a stranger. In those days no man would have dreamt of doing such a thing. They would not usually even talk to their own wife outside the house. For a rabbi to have an open conversation with a woman of such dubious character was a breach of all social, cultural and even religious rules. Had he no scruples?

What about Jesus' reputation? The truth is that reputation meant nothing to him; it was more important that he should reach people

> The harvest fields are still ripe for harvest. In fact, the worst times are the best time for evangelism because evangelism changes things.

with the good news. Paul told the Philippians, *"He made himself of no reputation"* (Philippians 2:7 NKJV). He jettisoned his reputation not only in associating with this woman and other such fringe characters; he did it when associating with us, when deciding to keep human company. He formed attachments to elements in the villages and towns that nobody else would look at. In fact, he made it his business to do so. The much-married Samaritan woman was typical. He knew that she was a sinner and yet he spoke to her as a favorite, giving us a clear example of his grace and openness.

God's Pattern of Action

They say birds of a feather flock together. Jesus was not of our feather but he did not hesitate to mingle with us. Christ receives sinful men – we need to grasp the tremendous implication of that fact. He made contacts as we all do, but for him it was part of the divine strategy. He made this point to the disciples, explaining to them that talking to this woman was what God had sent him to do, *"the will of him who sent me to finish his work"* (John 4:34). To Jesus it was *"food to eat that you know nothing about."* The woman had not given him the drink he had requested and he did not want the food the disciples had brought, but speaking to this Samaritan woman gave him the profound satisfaction of working directly with God. He had walked for two days to meet that woman – he knew he would and he went because *"the Son can do only what he sees his Father doing, because whatever the Father does the Son also does"* (John 5:19). In other words, the Father himself had sent his own Son on that walk to the dubious soul beside a well.

Throughout his entire career Jesus followed a pattern, the pattern of God's action described in the Old Testament. The Christ of the

New Testament was a copy of the God of the Old Testament (see, for example, Philippians 2 and Hebrews 1). God himself had rescued people like that woman long before. The Son had watched the Father restoring and showing mercy and love to the undeserving. It started with Adam and his wife Eve. An unforgettable instance was his mercy to King David, forgiving his terrible crime. We do not know whether David ever forgave himself but the realization that God still had room for him caused him to pen the most broken-hearted Psalm in the Bible. It is the most outstanding of Psalms, expressing a remarkable insight into the heart of God, well in advance of everyone else in those pre-Christian days: *"Let me hear joy and gladness. Hide your face from my sins and blot out all my iniquity. Then I will teach transgressors your ways, and sinners will turn back to you"* (Psalm 51:8-13).

The Son had seen God deal with King David, and now he did what the Father did, re-enacting ancient mercies, treating this sinful little woman as if she had never sinned. Although she was a sinner, he uttered no word to condemn her. It was always the same with him; he treated everybody whom he saved like that, for that is the way God always forgives. On that particular day in Samaria Jesus' actions initiated the salvation of a city. Today he still works like that and always will; as Luke explained in Acts 1:1, the Gospel accounts are of *"all that Jesus began to do and teach."* God is not a past God, an extinct volcano, and nor is he asleep: *"He who watches over Israel will neither slumber nor sleep"* (Psalm 121:4).

The greatest implication is that when we go out on our own saving mission, we are doing precisely what God commanded and does himself. It was Christ's joy and is our Christian joy. Here is the supreme way of life, to be part of the rolling greatness of eternal salvation. God works, and works with us. It is not an arduous task but a joyful one. As David said, joy is part of the message: *"Restore to me the joy of your salvation and I will teach transgressors your ways and sinners will turn back to you"* (Psalm 51:12-13). We are saved to serve and we are saved to save.

Timing

The next lesson from Sychar is about timing. Jesus said, *"I tell you, look at the fields! They are ripe for harvest"* (John 4:35). While he waited at the well, a crowd came out of the town, all men, dressed in white for coolness in the summer heat. They looked like a ripe harvest field, the sheaves of corn swaying in the breeze. In his Gospel, John gives ordinary situations a deeper significance. The white clothes suggested a harvest field – a spiritual one.

Jesus used a popular saying when talking to his disciples: *"Four months more and then the harvest?"* The saying meant that there was no need to hurry. We have similar sayings: "Rome wasn't built in a day", "more haste less speed" or perhaps even "mañana" as the Spanish say; there is always another day. It was typical of the low gear of the east and its slow-moving ways. Jesus took up the saying of his day but reversed it. He said, *"Do you not say, 'Four months more and then the harvest'? I tell you, open your eyes and look at the fields! They are ripe for harvest."* There was no time to waste!

> We are saved to serve and we are saved to save.

The woman at the well exemplified what he meant. She had gone harvesting. She really went for it. She was a bombshell! For her, the right time was at once. Jesus recognized her urgency and it triggered his comment: *"The sower and the reaper may be glad together"* (John 4:36) or as Amos prophesied, *"The days are coming, declares the Lord, when the reaper will be overtaken by the ploughman and the planter by the one treading grapes"* (Amos 9:13).

The harvest fields are still ripe for harvest. In fact, the worst times are the best time for evangelism because evangelism changes things. The gospel is the only real life-changing force. Conversions are better than the police force or law courts. *"Now is the day of salvation"* (2 Corinthians 6:2). Today is propitious; the Holy Spirit has no off days. The Samaritan woman did not worry about whether the time was right or not; she went ahead button-holing men on the street. The policies of the godless and human-ists breed national problems and they have to resort to draconian and restrictive laws to correct their own mistakes.

That nameless woman is our Bible example. She did not spend half her life getting ready, learning and learning again, ending up as a perpetual student. Jesus wants soul-savers who are keen to get on with the job; whether we are academics or illiterate, that is our task – to save the world. Some go on collecting qualifications, di-plomas and degrees, while lesser breeds gather in the harvest.

We learn most things – music, carpentry, art and swimming, for example – by practical application. That is the way to learn evange-lism. Jesus sent his disciples out on a trial mission with no time to get ready and they set off without a script, staff, money or a change of clothing. They never lacked anything and the very devils were subject to them. The experience taught them. Conferences, semi-nars and long prayer sessions have their place but their objective is to equip people to do God's work, and his work is salvation.

Gospel Entrepreneurs

In our Christ for all Nations campaign program we teach evange-lism to hundreds of thousand of Christian workers. We call these meetings our "Fire Conferences." There is a time to learn and a time to work. Turning things over in our minds ploughs no fields. Jesus was urgent but always unhurried. His instructions are to preach "as long as it is day" for tomorrow the curtain of night may fall on the stage. In wartime, air pilots were briefed on their mis-sion, questions asked and answered, then the commanding officer simply said, "Gentlemen, be airborne!"

The Samaritan woman was the world's first evangelist. She went to lead people to Jesus with the simple invitation *"Come, see a man!"* She had no Bible background but became an evangelist in the first hour she met Jesus. Jesus later commanded his disciples, *"You shall be my witnesses in Jerusalem, and in all Judea and Samaria"* (Acts 1:8). Samaria was the first place Jesus told them to go and the last place the disciples wanted to go. In fact, they did not go there; that was left to people who came along later. As those first disciples passed through Samaria with Jesus, they would have been happier to call down fire from heaven to destroy the place rather than preach in it.

Samaria was eventually evangelized by someone who had not heard Christ's Great Commission directly – a Greek-speaking man called Philip. The apostles had appointed him to look after widows when food was served but like the woman of Samaria he had "get up and go" in his soul. He slipped away and the apostles knew nothing about it until the news came of thousands being baptized, including a top-ranking Ethiopian official. Like the woman at the well, Philip had no supporters or organizations behind him. Like the woman at the well, Philip was a gospel entrepreneur. They each had a committee of two, themselves and the Holy Spirit.

Circumstances landed me in a similar situation. After coming to the end of our first African missionary effort, we had nobody to push us on and no financial backers. I was on my own, so the Holy Spirit had to be my sole reliance. Experience subsequently taught me never to do it any other way.

Agents of Christ

However, returning to the account in John 4, we can read Jesus' next lesson in evangelism. He said, *"The saying that 'one sows and another reaps', is true. I sent you to reap what you have not worked for. Others have done the hard work and you have reaped the benefits of their labor"* (John 4:37-38). Until then the disciples had done nothing much, so Jesus was anticipating future work. That is what I want to stress; even on virgin territory everything is prepared for us. Things are ready. The woman prepared the ground for Jesus in

Sychar and he was invited to spend two days with the Samaritans. The men of Sychar said to the woman, *"We no longer believe just because of what you said; now we have heard for ourselves, and we know that this man really is the Savior of the world"* (John 4:42). That was very good, but there's a slight sting in it. Men did not listen to women; they were considered nothing in those days. Yet the fact remains: Through her those men came to know Christ even if they discredited her part in the matter. She was the agent of Christ, whatever their attitude.

Philip went to Samaria about two years after Jesus had been there and built on the foundation that Jesus had laid, and *"there was great joy in that city"* (Acts 8:8). Evangelism is never really a lone effort. The Master is with us – as is the Holy Spirit – along with other allies, known or unknown, including angels. People's prayers of long ago are remembered and God answers those prayers through us as we work. God never forgets a prayer. He wants us to trust him. We do not need a postcard from heaven acknowledging receipt of our petition. What we pray always gets there safely, and no devil dare interfere with prayer in the name of Jesus.

In the Parable of the Net (Matthew 13) Jesus describes our evangelism as casting a net, flinging it over a stretch of water. The net stays there, bobbing along with the waves, with no sign of anything happening, but fish are entering it. When it is full, the fishers pull it to shore and sort out the catch, separating the good fish from the bad. It may seem as if nothing is happening as we go "fishing for men" but the Holy Spirit is at work even when there is no visible evidence. We should not be put off simply because we cannot see anything happening.

> Philip, Paul and Peter and all those wonderful people relied on us to carry on where they left off.

The early missionaries cut through the jungles of Africa to reach lost tribes and met with very little success. Since then hundreds of changes have taken place under historic influences. Today millions of people are anxious about the future and the only really clear answer is found in the gospel. Multitudes gather together, perhaps the largest crowds ever known, all hungry to hear the word of God. They have often known religion – the kind that advances with bloodshed and mayhem, the kind that demands a lot but offers nothing, the kind that is accompanied by fear and oppression. The difference is that the gospel brings us joy, freedom, peace, and hope. We have seen more people receive Christ in one day than the entire population of Rome in Paul's day. However, without the sacrifice and dedication of men and women over the past 150 years and more, I doubt whether we would see much happening today. We reap with joy where other men and women have labored with tears.

I find it is almost frightening, and certainly exciting, to think that Philip, Paul and Peter and all those wonderful people relied on us to carry on where they left off. Their burden has shifted to our shoulders, but thankfully so has their cloak of power.

Wages

Jesus went on to talk about wages. *"Even now the reaper draws his wages, even now he harvests the crop for eternal life"* (John 4:36). What we do we do for him, giving a helping hand to struggling men and women, but the *"laborer is worthy of his wages"* (1 Timothy 5:18). We serve the Lord Christ and he is a generous employer. If anyone works for cash, cash is what they will get, but Christ was not talking about a wage packet. The delight and joy of winning someone for Jesus is something nobody knows until it happens to them. Nothing sold in any store, nothing made in any factory, and no amount of money in a bank can give the same satisfaction as introducing somebody to Christ. We are not interested in adding their name to a paper list but in knowing that those names are engraved in the rock of eternity. It is an amazing thing that humans rather than angels are entrusted with the gospel.

Jesus is not looking for cheap labor; he is not interested in gaining what he can by paying dumping rates. *"The elders who direct the affairs of the church well are worthy of double honor"* (1 Timothy 5:17). The Greek word is *time*; it is used 41 times in the New Testament and usually translated "honor", but 9 times the translation is "price," which it can be here – "double price." The proper word for wages is actually *misthos*, but what does "double honor" mean to a worker kept poor? Malachi 3:5 tells us God's view, *"I will be quick to testify against those who defraud laborers of their wages."*

Jesus does not shun the word "wages." *"The reaper draws his wages,"* he said (John 4:36). God has a big and bountiful hand. *"He who goes out weeping, carrying seed to sow, will return with songs of joy, carrying sheaves with him"* (Psalm 126:6). How marvelous that there is such a calling, to introduce people to Jesus, bless them, bring them into the love of the family of God, and make them our friends!

Where there is sacrifice, Jesus said, it will be returned a hundred-fold (Mark 10:30). St. Francis of Assisi called men to a life of poverty. Yet Jesus never did that. He sent disciples on a mission and asked them whether they lacked anything on their travels, and they said, "No." He is the most generous of Masters. He is the King and gives in royal fashion.

Questions

1. Evangelism brings its own reward but would you work harder if it put cash in your pocket?
2. What allies have you in evangelism?

I no longer call you servants,
because a servant does not know his master's business.
Instead, I have called you friends for everything I learned
from my Father I have made known to you.

John 15:15

CHAPTER 4

Slaving for God?

"I no longer call you servants. I have called you friends."

John 15:15

We do not become Christians by shouldering a load of extra demands. Christ is the burden bearer not the burden giver. *"Come to me, all you who are weary and burdened, and I will give you rest"* (Matthew 11:28). Whatever we do to please him is futile if it is a drag and chore.

Witnessing for Christ is not witnessing to our own piety, nor is it witnessing to a life of dos and don'ts, building fences for people to climb over to reach Christ. Scripture pictures the Christian life as a race but not as a mountaineering expedition. Preaching salvation is not about preaching a sanctification program.

We are all aware of our shortcomings but some people are anxious and even apologetic to God. Their Christian experience is heavy going. They seem to have a Lord who is exacting and critical and who blesses their work reluctantly because of their faults and flaws. They are worried that they may have grieved God or missed his will in some way.

Is the Lord like that, irritably demanding the impossible? My Lord is not. We are told to approach him "boldly" – not apologetically – and to enter his courts with praise and exuberance, expecting a hearty welcome. Our songs should not be lamenting but throbbing with the rhythm of coming into our own home, where the Father himself is at the door waiting for us. In his presence is fullness of joy – for us and him. Satan, the *"accuser of our brothers,"* loves to intimidate us, to paint false pictures of our relationship with God. God's eyes are holy but Christ *"has become for us our righteousness, holiness and redemption"* (1 Corinthians 1:30). We do not need to grovel, lowering ourselves like conquered captives, adopting abject names, calling ourselves "vile sinners" or "dust." I do not sing, "I'm only a sinner saved by grace." I am not only a sinner any more. I am not crawling around under the guilt of being reminded that I am an ex-sinner, like a criminal on bail. I have been justified by grace and am treated as if I had never sinned, a newborn, chosen, and cherished child of God. *"Who is he that condemns?"* (Romans 8:34).

Far from wondering whether God will listen to us, we need to hear what he is saying. He calls us to work beside him. Christ offers us service as a noble privilege, not toil and dullness. He is our role model. He said, *"My Father is always at his work and I, too, am working. The Son of Man did not come to be served but to serve"* (John 5:17, Matthew 20:28). Work is God-like and life's obligations are meant to be an unbroken act of love. God is not our employer and we are not employees, underlings, paid hands. We have a share in the family business. Jesus said, *"I must be about my Father's business"* (Luke 2:49 NKJV), and his business is our business.

Love as the Basis of Service

Christ's teaching on service is illustrated in John 15:9-17. His first remarks are typical of his insistence on love. *"As the Father has loved me, so have I loved you. My command is this: love each other as I have loved you"* (vv 9+12).

> We do not become Christians by shouldering a load of extra demands. Christ is the burden bearer not the burden giver.

Love as the basis of service is emphasized in Scripture. Our first example is taken from the Old Testament, the account in Genesis of Jacob serving 7 years for the love of beautiful Rachel. In Exodus 21:2-6, immediately after the law established by the Ten Commandments God gave a new law concerning love-based work. It illustrates the truth that love fulfils the law. The Exodus picture is of a man working off a debt by serving his creditor. He was not to work for longer than 6 years and during that time he was free to marry and have children. However, his family was legally owned by the man he served. In the 7th year, he could go free but could not take his family with him. If he loved his family and wanted to stay with them, he had to become a servant-slave for life. He would give himself **to** his master **for** the love of his wife and family.

This rule of Moses foreshadows Christ. In the Exodus law, the man wishing to serve for life would be brought to the door and his ear pierced with a bradawl, leaving a permanent scar so that everyone could tell that he was serving for the love of his wife and family. Christ also gave himself **to** God **for** us, for ever. Christ, too, was pierced for us. In Revelation he appears bearing the mark of the wounds that he suffered for us. Without love, obeying commands is a treadmill of duty. Love makes service a pleasure. Labor becomes as affectionate as an embrace.

Friends of Jesus

In his discourse Jesus takes it even further. *"Greater love has no one than this, that he lay down his life for his friends"* (John 15:13). His words are inscribed on war memorials and cenotaphs all over the world.

Why did Jesus say "friends"? Wouldn't it be even greater love to die for enemies? The answer lies in what Jesus meant by "friend". It is more than the ordinary friendship of a companion. The word in Greek is *philos*. At his arrest Jesus called Judas "friend", using the word *hetairos* (a clansman) not *philos*. Jesus used it with the overtone of irony, making it clear that Judas was not the kind of close friend that Scripture so often talks about. The *philoi* friends of Jesus were specially distinguished people, people with a special capacity.

The Old Testament contains several examples of friends who held a privileged position: *"Zabud the son of Nathan, a priest and the king's friend"* (1 Kings 4:5 NKJV; NIV: personal adviser); *"Amnon had a friend named Jonadab, a very shrewd man"* (2 Samuel 13:3); and *"Hushai, the Arkite, David's friend"* (2 Samuel 16:16). These were official "friends," not royalty but counselors living close to rulers, chosen men. Jesus said to his disciples, *"I chose you"* (John 15:16). That is, as his "friends." That Scripture has nothing to do with being chosen to be saved for heaven but chosen as a friend, to serve in a special capacity. In days gone by, a ruler would sometimes choose a young boy to be brought up with his own son, the prince and the boy growing together in intimate companionship. He was chosen to share the young prince's problems, secrets and thoughts, especially when the son took his royal father's place. He would be his personal counselor, knowing him thoroughly, knowing the state secrets and affairs, always close to the king, and a power behind the throne.

When Jesus said *"I no longer call you servants, but friends,"* that is the kind of friend he was talking about. Abraham was a friend like that to God (see 2 Chronicles 20:7) and God conferred with the patriarch about his intentions. *"The Lord said, 'Shall I hide from Abraham what I am about to do?'"* (Genesis 18:17). God made another friend 400 years later – Moses: *"The Lord would speak to Moses face to face, as a man speaks with his friend. He made known his ways to Moses"* (Exodus 33:11, Psalm 103:7). The theme of God's friendship runs through Scripture. The prophets are God's friends: *"Surely the Sovereign Lord does nothing without revealing his plan to his servants the prophets"* (Amos 3:7).

Jesus now establishes the same confidentiality with human beings. He opened up spiritual secrets to the disciples saying, *"I no longer call you servants, because a servant does not know his master's business. Instead, I have called you friends for everything I learned from my Father I have made known to you"* (John 15:15). In fact, he even divulged secrets about himself to women, and women had never been trusted like that in those days.

Soulwinners *"have the mind of Christ"* (1 Corinthians 2:16). Our call is to know God's mind and to preach it as God's ambassadors. We simply convey the message. It is not our own message but the heart-call of God. Paul said that God had entrusted him with the gospel, making him a debtor to all nations until he had delivered God's message to them. The word of God enlightens our understanding and the Holy Spirit writes the word in letters of fire in our soul, giving us the authority to speak it. Change or dilute it and it becomes ashes.

To know God's mind is not to gather information, a collection of facts simply to be understood. God sends his word to accomplish his purpose, an effective living force. There is no other book like the Bible. No other words ever written have an inherent power to affect us. They affect the messenger first and then the messenger's hearers, bringing them into line with the message. The Bible defends itself. It does not mind critics for it criticizes them. Jesus said, *"If you obey my commands* [to love one another], *you will remain in my love"* (John 15:10). That is his promise. He said, *"The words I have spoken to you are spirit and they are life"* (John 6:63). He speaks of love and his words create love; he wraps us in garments woven on the loom of eternal love.

The King dying for the Servant

In saying *"Greater love has no man than this that he lay down his life for his friends,"* Jesus was making an amazing statement. A king's friend would be expected to risk his life for him. Scripture gives us the example of Hushai, friend and counselor to David. When Absalom rebelled and tried to steal the throne from his father, Hushai curried favor with Absalom and was included in his war counsel. He learned Absalom's plans and strategies and used a grapevine chain of people to take the insider knowledge to David. It was a very risky undertaking. One of the runners was almost caught. David had other friends at that time but Hushai risked his life by carrying out that particular mission.

Apart from Hushai, a whole Israeli army was ready to fight to the death for David. He wanted to join them and lead his troops but they said no: *"You must not go out. You are worth ten thousand of us"* (2 Samuel 18:3). Israel's thousands were prepared to lay down their lives for King David but would not allow David to risk his life for them – that would have been unthinkable.

Jesus is our David, the one worthy and worth living and dying for. Millions have done that and still do so today, as witnesses, confessors and martyrs. That is as it should be. Many died for David and many have died for Christ, David's greater son.

What would be utterly wrong would be for a king to die for his army or to fling himself in front of his bodyguard and take a fatal thrust. We need to adjust our thinking to appreciate the astounding truth of the gospel: Christ laid down his life for his friends – for us, who should have laid down our lives for him. *"Very rarely will anyone die for a righteous man, though for a good man someone might possibly dare to die. But God demonstrates his own love for us in this: while we were still sinners, Christ died for us"* (Romans 5:7).

God's Heart Cry from Calvary

This makes popular religious belief today look ridiculous. "Do good and be kind," they say; all religions come to the same thing. Where does Christ come in? What about this tremendous fact, that Christ came down to earth and gave his life for us? If we only needed to be kind and good, why did he make that sacrifice? Was it a tragic mistake? What amazing presumption! Ordinary men and women brushing aside the gospel as nothing, the core belief of millions across 2,000 years! It is the central focus of the word of God. Our own ideas simply do not compare. Here is the historic demonstration of truth. The gospel is the rock that never rocks. Calvary is the voice of God and evangelism is God's heart cry from Calvary.

We live for Jesus, but Jesus lives for us. He is not a "good cause" – we are! We think of helping him but he helps us. We defend him but he defends us. The story is not that we came to his aid but that he came to ours: *"You did not choose me, but I chose you"* (John 15:16). We did not elect him as Lord. He elects us. We are not "building his kingdom" for he gives it to us: *"Do not be afraid, little flock, for your Father has been pleased to give you the king-dom"* (Luke 12:32). We shall never crown him King of Kings but crowns of righteousness have been set aside for the faithful.

He deserves better than we can ever give him. When we have done everything, we have only done what we can. What we achieve is nothing when we remember what he achieved for us. The yoke is his yoke and he carries the heavy end. We were his enemies but he calls us "friends." For him service meant dying on a cross.

Workers together with Him

Jesus served and taught us to serve in times when half the population were slaves. Rome had a slave economy. Greatness was counted by the number of slaves that waited on you. The great were the good by Roman standards. Slaves did everything, learned lan-guages and exercised skills. The soldier race, Sparta, treated farming people almost as cockroaches. Jesus' teaching of love-based service was a revolution.

> The gospel is the rock that never rocks. Calvary is the voice of God and evangelism is God's heart cry from Calvary.

A thousand years before Greece, God commanded Israel *"6 days you shall labor"* (Exodus 12:9). Pagans worked 7 days a week but Israel had a rest day. They were the world's first free nation. How-ever, God wanted Israel to serve him, not to be idle and be looked after by captive slaves. God himself works and wants us to be like him. All Jews acquired a trade or some form of usefulness. Paul and

Aquila were tentmakers and Jesus himself was a tekton, a carpenter or possibly a general builder. It was written of him *"Here I am, I have come – it is written about me in the scroll. I desire to do your will, O my God; your law is within my heart"* (Psalm 40:7). That obedience meant 20 years as a workman, three years of ministry and then his redeeming death. He became a servant to servants.

Jesus lived to serve. There was no point in his coming to earth as far as gain was concerned. For him there was none: *"The Son of Man did not come to be served, but to serve, and to give his life as a ransom for many"* (Matthew 20:28). "To serve" or "to minister" means work; the Greek word used here is *diakoneo*, to work for others. Jesus was a "deacon". He gained nothing and we gained everything. Jesus was born for us, lived for us, taught for us, healed for us, died for us, rose for us, ascended to God for us and is coming again for us. He took nothing and gave everything and had no reward except wounds. Though God exalted him, it was to place him back where he had been before.

People speak of Christ's passion and the appalling violence that he endured, but he had something to be passionate about – the plight of a lost world. His service was unpaid and infinitely costly: *"He poured out his life unto death"* (Isaiah 53:12). If service involves no sacrifice, what is it worth? If it is as easy as sitting in a fireside chair, has it any true value? David said, *"I will not offer to the Lord my God burnt offerings that cost me nothing"* (2 Samuel 24:24). Paul said, *"Even if I am being poured out like a drink offering on the sacrifice and service coming from your faith, I am glad and rejoice with you all"* (Philippians 2:17). Paul "pouring out" himself for those early Christians is a picture to challenge us. He took the example of his Master, who *"made himself nothing"* (Philippians 2:7) and who *"loved us and gave himself up for us as a fragrant offering and sacrifice to God"* (Ephesians 5:2). The horror of the cross echoes through Psalm 22:14: *"I am poured out like water."* We sing of our sacrifice of praise, but how much sacrifice is that?

A sidelight on the new attitude to work is found in Acts 28:3 showing Paul the apostle, known to kings, gathering sticks or brushwood for a fire. Only women did that sort of thing. They were the drudges. Christ changed that. Women and men perform their tasks for him, Jesus.

Love is goodness. Love is the ultimate motive. Love is the joy and privilege of stooping to Jesus' feet to render the slightest service. He deserves better than we can ever give him. We do all we can, but it is precious little. Nonetheless, we should do what we can. What we achieve is nothing when we think of his worthy greatness. Our incredible privilege is that he calls us alongside him to help shoulder his cross. Then he calls us "friends."

Questions

1. What is the Judeo-Christian work ethic?
2. What should be our attitude to work?

You are worthy,
our Lord and God, to receive glory and honor and power,
for you created all things, and by your will they
were created and have their being.

Revelation 4:11

CHAPTER 5

That's God's Business

"I must be about my Father' business."
Luke 2:49 NKJV

Witness and evangelism are a lifetime appointment. We are not casual labor, employed by God to help out when we have nothing better to do. It is not by chance that we do what we do but a "holy calling."

When he was 12 years old, Jesus was on a visit to Jerusalem and went missing from the pilgrim party. His mother Mary found him and said, *"Your father and I have been anxiously searching for you"* (Luke 2:48). Jesus replied, *"I must be about my Father's business"* and then went back home to be about Joseph's business as a *tekton*, which is usually translated as carpenter. He continued as a humble workman for 18 years and God expressed his delight at the beginning of Christ's ministry saying, *"This is my son, whom I love; with him I am well pleased"* (Matthew 3:16). Jesus always was "about his Father's business" even when he was about Joseph's business. As Paul said to slaves, *"It is the Lord Christ you are serving"* (Colossians 3:24). Whatever we do for a living, our true career is our Father's business.

God is at work. This world is the arena of his saving operations but we are also called in to serve and to share God's world concern. Measured alongside his interests, how do our activities look? He gives and gives. The way of the world is to get and get.

God wants us to jump on his chariot, be his men and women at arms, with the devil lying crushed beneath his chariot wheels. We need look no further for the meaning of life. There is no higher fulfillment than to take salvation to our generation. It also makes

There is no higher fulfillment than to take salvation to our generation.

the world a better place, but that is incidental to the true work of salvation with its eternal outcome.

Now I am not talking about a kind of hobby. Nor are we gospel entertainers, showmen. The quality of preaching in church is unfortunately often judged by whether people enjoy it or not. Yet this can be to miss the point. The true test of the validity of the message preached is its truth and its impact on people's lives. God complained in Ezekiel's prophecy, saying, *"To them you are nothing more than one who sings love songs with a beautiful voice and plays an instrument well, for they hear your words but do not put them into practice"* (Ezekiel 33:32). Meanwhile, as we now well know, the destiny of the 10 tribes hung on whether they paid attention. They did not and vanished in the crucible of the nations. We must sense the importance of our message. What counts are not our thoughts and ideas but God bringing everyone to the bar of his truth. Sooner or later the word clashes with the ungodly world.

In ordinary life we value the gifts and skills of entertainers, men and women of sporting prowess, the genius of music, drama, wit and the theatre. However, the show ends, like a good meal, and nothing has changed. Our pleasures bring relief like aspirin, which stops the pain but "does not affect the heart" as the commercials say. The true gospel is medicine that "affects the heart" – positively. Christian witness runs through the world like a refreshing stream renewing everything it touches – people, the world, the future and even heaven, filling it with the redeemed.

The Message is not measured by the Messenger

Gospel wisdom is not the wisdom of the one who carries it. It is the wisdom of God. We may go about the task in fear and trembling like Paul in Corinth, but the word is a hammer that shatters the rock. Jesus quoted Psalm 8:2: *"From the lips of children and infants you have ordained praise."* Anyone who hears the word of God and speaks it is a bastion of the truth. Moses was not convinced that the people would listen to him, let alone do what he said, but in the end even the mighty sea reacted to his voice and the waters fled when he spoke with God's authority.

In our previous chapters we referred to Moses and his exploits as God set about freeing the slaves of Egypt. The astonishing thing is that God could even contemplate using Moses as a possible leader. Brought up as a royal Egyptian, he made a hash of his opportunities, murdered a man and had to get away quickly. For 40 years he was reduced to being a sheep-minder, a job even a boy could do. Then the day came when God called him to embark on a historic career.

Moses is typical of the people used by God. All through Scripture and ever since, apparently unfit people have become outstanding servants of God. There is neither time nor room here to begin the 4,000-year-old list of little people whom God used in a big way. Come to think of it, who really is fit for the divine task, anyway?

Many are waiting to feel that they have grown up enough and have credentials and sufficient spirituality. Some struggle to be "an empty vessel" but do not know how to go about it or even what being "empty" means – especially as the promise of God is to fill us, not empty us. A song often sung prays, "Break me, melt me, mold me, fill me!" After a filling experience, what then? Pray it again? Is that what is needed? Time is short and there is not a moment to lose.

There is no way of testing or measuring our spiritual stature; while we are growing, we can get on with the work. David was just an immature and brash adolescent when God used him to sling a stone that won a battle. If we are not careful, piety can degenerate into self-concern, causing us to focus on saving our own soul. Spirituality does not always go hand in hand with God's call to faith-filled action. Concentrating on our own "perfections" tends

> God saves only those who know that he saves, but nobody knows unless we tell them (Romans 10:14). If we do what we can, he will do what we cannot. Do the possible and he does the impossible.

to make us compare ourselves with others. Often others are forging ahead doing things for God and they become targets of our criticism – a distinct flaw in our self-satisfied spirituality.

The reward of holiness is to be holy not powerful. The degree of power we have has nothing to do with the degree of our virtue. Power is not a reward but a gift of unmerited grace, given by the Holy Spirit; the Holy Spirit is received by faith not earned by something we do (see Galatians 3:2). If God's power was dispensed in proportion to perfection, who would even dare to stake a claim?

What Moses accomplished changed the world for all time, despite his shortcomings. It was astonishing. He served God in many ways – perhaps because no one else was available. Apart from freeing slaves, he was, for example, the first to demonstrate the power of the name of the Lord. Moses unfurled a banner emblazoned with the divine name, the logo of heaven. Moses' prophetic calling is the calling of every born-again believer today. He also proved that the Lord is the friend and champion of the oppressed and a foe of tyrants. Today we stand in the succession of Moses and are sent into the world to prove that same thing.

When believers are casual about the work of evangelism, it is generally because they do not think that it matters much or they are not "that up to it." They feel God is Almighty and can do it all himself; he does not particularly need us. It may be difficult to believe, but that is not how God wants things to work. He created us to be his hands on earth. God is working, but leaves it entirely to us to take the gospel to the world. If we fail, he has no "Plan B". It is up to us.

The Creator established the order and set us here to be the instruments through which his plans are brought to fruition. If the work is to be done, it will be done with us or not at all. There is a reason for that. God has special joy when the godless turn to him and, as he loves us, his aim is to bless us with the same divine level of joy. The invitation is *"Come and share your master's happiness!"* (Matthew 25:21,23). The Lord means us to succeed – and enjoy it.

A friend told me that when he was about four years old, his father, a carpenter, used a two-wheeled handcart to carry wood and tools around in. Sometimes he would take the little boy on the cart with him. One day my friend wanted to help to push the cart. So, when they had nearly reached their destination, his father set him down, put his small hands on the cart and told him he could help to push. The people at the house saw them arriving and Dad proudly told them how his son had "helped". A four-year-old does not walk very fast and does not have the strength to push a heavy cart. Dad could have managed better and quicker without his son. However, there was a principle at work; for my friend's father, the satisfaction of seeing his son's delight was more important than speed.

The Almighty wants our hands on the cart. Moses could not create the plagues of Egypt, but he called them down. He had no power over winds and water but the sea parted at his command. As one man on his own, Moses could not defeat an Egyptian military brigade but with God he did just that – quite a change of role for a shepherd. *"Salvation comes from the Lord"* (John 2:9), but the Lord never operates solo. He chooses volunteers to work with him. God saves only those who know that he saves, but nobody knows unless we tell them (Romans 10:14). If we do what we can, he will do what we cannot. Do the possible and he does the impossible.

> The God of deliverance sent Moses and now sends us with the same message: *"Let my people go!"*

Fearless Audacity

Look again at that great Biblical example of a servant of God, Moses. He was the meekest man on earth but clearly not the bravest. He had no army; Israel was still only a rabble of tribes. Yet Moses snatched Pharaoh's entire slave force and their livestock from under his royal nose, *"not a hoof was to be left behind"* (Exodus 10:26). Joining forces with a God like that, Moses showed fearless audacity and drive. God took away the heart of a rabbit and gave him the heart of a lion instead.

Moses did what he did with such aplomb and flair that it became world news. His crook still in his hand and wearing his stained shepherd's coat, he walked straight from the field of sheep into Pharaoh's throne room. He passed through one guarded gate after another and a whole series of studded palace doors until he reached the glittering splendor of the presence of Pharaoh. This was a nobody whom God made a somebody with a peremptory, uncompromising message: *"Let my people go!"* Pharaoh and his court stared at this daring man who was clearly no diplomat. I expect they laughed. But God was on the warpath and the most powerful ruler on earth stood no chance against Moses – and God.

The God of deliverance sent Moses and now sends us with the same message: *"Let my people go!"* Our witness and evangelism are efforts that the world despises and pretends to ignore, but we attract the backing of God. Paul said he was *"known, yet regarded as unknown"* (2 Corinthians 6:9). He could tell King Agrippa that nothing of what he had gone through had been *"done in a corner"* (Acts 26:26). Our stand for God is known and is a flea in the ear of the world. It tries not to notice but it does.

The Queen of England bestowed no knighthood on Wesley, Whitfield or any famous evangelist but they had the attention of someone far more important, the Lord himself. Someone once phoned the church attended by the US President and asked if he would be there that morning. The reply was that they did not know whether the President would be there but they did expect God – which the caller might consider of far greater importance.

The church is operating on a global scale. Believers whom we have never seen are our allies. Flotsam and jetsam on the shores of continents are being salvaged for which no other organization caters. All people are savable because God made them to be saved. The gospel is his plan for everyone on earth; even the worst offender is not denied hope. Hell is not designed for crowds. Heaven is expecting them! Nobody is created for burning.

We can take further encouragement also from Moses, the first agent of deliverance. He felt totally inadequate. Israel's leaders would not listen to him, he thought. Indeed, why should they? To them Moses must have seemed an unknown in his declining years, suffering from crazed hallucinations that God had sent him to defy all Egypt and take Pharaoh's entire slave force off to a land of milk and honey. As for God sending him, it was no God they knew and certainly not one of the popular Egyptian gods.

Yet the Lord equipped Moses with convincing evidence. He overcame their doubts and every Hebrew slave followed him out of Egypt. They were only half-civilized, in fact turbulent and idolatrous, agitated by truculent characters, ungrateful for Moses concern, and even resenting him for uprooting and dragging them out of Egypt with his airy promise. Tragically for them, God heard their criticisms and gave them what they actually had no problem believing – that they would never see Canaan. They all died on its very borders. It was the next generation that marched in with victory shouts.

Today God sends us out just as he sent Moses to release the devil's captives and change the world. We may have a sense of inferiority and ask, "Who are we? What qualifications do we have?" Well, Moses had none and asked exactly the same question, *"Who am I?"*

God replied that what counted was not who Moses was but who he was – and he was going to be there (Exodus 3:11-12). We may be undistinguished, just "that church lot"! Television makes fun of us in comedy programs where we feature as zealous "religion pushers," and newspapers have no ink to spare for church affairs. Criminals are news but not when they become Christians. But what does it matter? God does not watch the television or read newspapers.

The church is God's Moses today, equipped and given credentials by the Holy Spirit and sent to challenge the world and its ways. God sent prophets like Isaiah to people he knew would not listen. We may sometimes feel like Isaiah, speaking to people who are unwilling to hear. But this is the day of the Holy Spirit. We go out at Christ's bidding and we have the joy of seeing sinners repent. Do what God says and he does what we say. When God says go, he gives us going power. Those who refuse the word will end up like scraps on the floor of the designer's cutting room.

Share your Master's Happiness

In John's vision described in Revelation, he saw an open door in heaven and scenes of unsurpassed glory. In Chapter 4 he says that 24 "elders", beings of unknown splendor, sat arrayed on their awesome thrones. They were joined by four "living creatures", great immortal spirits, drawn from far-off dimensions of the angelic world. They all worshipped God. First they worshipped him as the Creator. *"You are worthy, our Lord and God, to receive glory and honor and power, for you created all things, and by your will they were created and have their being"* (Revelation 4:11). Then, in Chapter 5, John saw this dazzling choir augmented by endless multitudes: *"Then I looked and heard the voice of many angels, numbering thousands upon thousands and ten thousand times ten thousand. In a loud voice they sang, 'Worthy is the Lamb who was slain.' Then I heard every creature in heaven and on earth and under the earth and on the sea, and all that is in them, singing, 'To him who sits on the throne and to the Lamb, be praise and honor and glory and power, for ever and ever"* (Revelation 5:11-13). Worship of the Creator turned to worship of the Lamb, the Deliverer, who redeemed us when we were hostage to sin. He paid our ransom at the cost of his own outpoured life blood.

Those worship scenes are there to enthuse and encourage us. They show what the true end is, a preview of what our witness will produce. The redeemed crowd the streets of the City of God, while angels stand aside. You will be there, and I, if we follow the Lamb. We will be in the same multitude that John saw, standing with Peter who preached the first gospel sermon on the day of Pentecost, and Philip, the first to cross over to Gentile territory to preach Jesus – and with Paul the apostle, Luther, Wesley, missionaries, evangelists, pastors, scholars, mothers, fathers, songwriters, and all who have ever told the story of Jesus and his love. These are the worthy, God's heroes, their voices joined together like the music of many waters, streams of hope. Nobody can be forgotten. Love's labor is never lost. Paradise regained. Joy like ocean waves, lofty cadences echoing through vast celestial architecture and to the uttermost bounds of creation – choirs, orchestras and mighty organs all rejoicing in the Lamb who is our Savior and Deliverer!

The Lamb said, *"Follow me and I will make you fishers of men"* (Matthew 4:19). If our road does not converge with his road, it leads nowhere.

Salvation is of the Lord and vain is the help of princes, yet he calls us to be involved in saving the world and to share his joy: "Come and share your master's happiness!" I cannot think of anything greater to do; no privilege surpasses it.

Questions

1. This chapter mentions Moses as God's special agent.
   Can you name any other Bible characters who were agents?
2. Why does God call for our help?

Africa Is Being Saved!

Miracle healings that amaze modern science
are part of the signs-following Gospel.

1,046,390 souls record a decision for Christ in five days of meetings.
On Target for One Hundred Million Souls this Decade!

At every crusade, prayer partners' requests are brought in
and prayed for by all in attendance!

Abuja

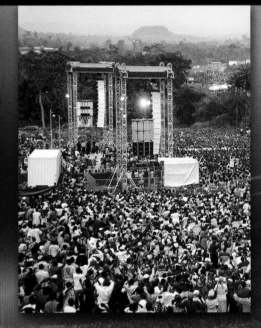

Giant sound towers make it possible for people to hear the Gospel, even miles away.

Up to 820,000 people gathered in a single meeting.

Evangelist Bonnke severs the chains of a 25-year old, healed from insanity.

ADO-EKITI

IBADAN

1.3 million attend a single service at the Ibadan Great Gospel Crusade.

LAGOS, NIGERIA

During the five day campaign, over 3.4 million people registered their salvation decisions and a staggering 1.6 million people attended a single service! CfaN books have been translated into 138 languages and over 178 million copies have been printed in 53 countries.

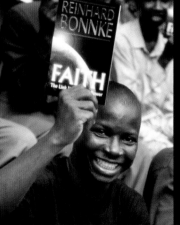

Follow-up forms an important part of each campaign – each new believer is given a copy of the booklet *Now That You Are Saved* and integrated into a local church.

A former Nigerian Paralympics competitor, confined to his tricycle wheelchair for three years, could now walk!

Jos, Nigeria

In five days of meetings, over 1.2 million people made registered decisions for Jesus Christ!

During the Ogbomosho Great Gospel Crusade, 1,758,144 souls were gloriously saved.

Ogbomosho

Local musicians and singers lead the crowd in joyous praise and worship.

Ayangba

Over half a million responded to the call of salvation and registered their decision during the five days of meetings.

Forbidding clouds and the torrential rain that followed could not keep this crowd from gathering to hear the Gospel preached, worshipping joyfully, or rejoicing in miracles.

Alongside every crusade, Evangelist Reinhard Bonnke shares at a Fire Conference during the daytime to equip and inspire church leaders and workers for Holy Spirit evangelism. At the Jos Fire Conference, 50,000 gathered for "a flame for every head!"

Part 2

I know that the Lord saves his anointed;
he answers him from his holy heaven with
the saving power of is right hand.

Psalm 20:6

CHAPTER 6

Fads?

"That by all possible means we might save some."

1 Corinthians 9:22

The first gospel evangelism in Europe took place at a women's meeting by the river. On the next occasion the preachers were in the stocks in jail. Things do not necessarily need to be that difficult, although Paul and Silas certainly won converts that way.

Did those first evangelists know how to go about winning converts in pagan Europe? Jesus said, "Go!" but gave no further instructions. The Acts of the Apostles depicts a remarkable strategy and Holy Spirit guidance but the apostles had to find their own approach.

Acts 16:11-15 describes how they first set out from Antioch in Syria. This was Paul's second foreign trip, but this time he traveled from east to west, from Asia to Europe, involving a two-day crossing of the Aegean from Troas to Macedonia. He and his companions made their way to Philippi, a Roman colony in Macedonia, and spent a few days getting to know the city. They learned that Jewish and other women met for prayer at a place by the river and on the Sabbath they made their way there through the city gate.

Few Jewish people lived in that area. Ten men could open a synagogue but women were debarred from doing the same. However, they could pray anywhere. The disciples sat down with them by the river and talked about Jesus. That day they had the first Christian convert in Europe, a business woman named Lydia. She and her household were baptized and she invited the apostles to stay in her home for a while. Paul continued to go to the prayer spot by the river and one day encountered a fortune-teller who followed them shouting about who they were. She had a spirit of divination and Paul expelled it. For his trouble he and Silas landed in jail. Then the famous story of the earthquake and the conversion of the jailor took place.

That is how the West began to be won for God. Those first evangelists sought and grasped one slim opportunity for God. It was hardly the custom then for two men to sit down by a river and talk to women; nor, for that matter, was singing to God in a dungeon at midnight. It was also a new idea to shout out a gospel sentence in the dark. Those intrepid pioneers were not worried about custom or church tradition. Any opportunity anywhere would do. By their enterprise and imaginative boldness they penetrated the pagan world of ancient superstitions.

Today life and culture has been Christianized and is totally different. Church routine is familiar throughout the world. The work of God usually seems to be church work, maintaining some place as a gospel centre. That may be held to be the best way to work but it is certainly not the only way.

Church custom may render "the gospel service" the only method and even establish the time of it, 6:30 each Sunday evening, as if it was part of the law handed down at Sinai. It is so often a case of preaching to the converted and as devoid of potential as going fishing in the kitchen sink. It qualifies a church as evangelical, although it contrasts starkly with the fact that no apostle ever preached in a Christian building.

I do not wish to discount any method. My point is simply that the enterprise of Paul and Silas in Philippi is an example and challenge. Great historic figures such as Paul, Peter, Silas and Barnabas risked going to places to talk about Jesus knowing that they could be thrown out ignominiously. In fact, Paul's routine experience seems to have been a round of synagogue riots and revivals. The world knew nothing about Jesus and his great work of salvation and the early Christians talked about it wherever they happened to be. Their methods and means were whatever they could do wherever they were. It was news and they were full of it, bright eyed and eager.

It is often said that God uses men not methods. That is a half truth. God uses men who use methods. Without some approach, nothing gets done; we have to evangelize one way or other.

To think creatively we must think laterally, or so the experts tell us. Thinking for the gospel needs to be creative; *"love – with all your mind"* (Matthew 22:37). Evangelism is the big business of kingdom economy, with many features and approaches. Each person has his or her own role within the church's programs of evangelism and alone as they go about their daily affairs. Can we do it better?

The evangelistic drive may be for us to stand up, open Bible in hand, and preach to a multitude hanging on to our every word. We know that few indeed will fulfill such an ambition, but evangelism can represent a thousand opportunities if we make the most of every opening with the gospel. Everything we are could be called up in the service of God, and that includes inventive thought, imagination, and energetic action. It need not be the pastor, leader, or church board introducing changes and means. Churches have many gifted men and women, successful in their own fields, and their know-how and ability could help to direct churches in their general outreach.

Churches and church organizations have sometimes employed schemes devised by advertising agencies. The drawback is that secular promotion generally has no experience of "selling" a "product" such as the gospel. Their usual wares are things people would want, whereas the gospel has more to overcome than sales resistance, including outright hostility at times. That is where the Christian confrontation in a spirit of love is likely to be the best approach.

From time to time new church methods become fashionable. If they seem adaptable, they can be taken up. However, what is successful in one area or with certain leadership and enthusiasm may not be appropriate in different circumstances. It is worth trying anything that has been successful in spreading the gospel. Church practices have often become sacrosanct traditions, kept alive by exertion and determination long after they have ceased to be fruitful. This is justified as being "faithful." Well, we can be faithful in a rut.

Schemes and techniques have followed one another in evangelistic churches like the seasons. They have been labeled as "fads." Any one of them may have started out as a new idea put forward by Holy Spirit energized and enthusiastic workers but those who take up the baton need the same drive and enthusiasm. Methods need manpower and are only effective to the extent that they inspire effort. They will not work like machines on their own.

Of course, not all new ideas are sensible and can be the result of individual interpretations of random verses from the Bible. A colleague of mine once received a series of letters declaring that the "failure" of the church today was due to women cutting their hair or not wearing hats in worship. The idea was that God would let souls go to perdition because churchwomen went to the hairdressers'. Jesus said that he was sending his disciples into a world of wolves and that they would need the wisdom of serpents.

Then there are the "prophets" with their own private hotline to God; they like to tell us "what the Lord is saying to the church" as if they are revealing a great secret: "Do this and revival will come; crowds will cram the pews." Groups insisting that God has shown them that their way is the true pattern have caused divisions over practices and church structures and weakened support for the united testimony. Disillusionment comes too late and the sectarian divisions continue.

The church is not a society for the preservation of ancient customs. We work for God not for systems; we are not machine attendants. New ways are not wrong simply because they are new. The circumstances, changes in cultures and fashion make constant demands on Christian thought in order to meet the need. Some give up trying new ways because they have not yielded the expected results. Those methods may have promised too much but they could still be useful. It is better to try new things than stick to traditions which have been seen to produce little in return for all the hard work. We have to use our minds and test all things.

The crux of the matter is that it is widely assumed that there must be a right method or a good means which will yield a harvest and make the whole evangelistic enterprise so much easier. Some believe that praying it is the answer, ushering in what they call revival; others think that praise is the key; others still advocate standing in worship ... or using new songs, introducing new church structures, new organization, or new Bible teaching – something must hold the great secret to shepherding the masses into the Christian fold. This is pure speculation but some are so sure of it that they search Scripture for the missing technique or formula and cry "Eureka!" if they hit on a something that backs their view. The fact is that the Scriptures never say that there is a panacea like that. They never encourage us to suppose that one fixed approach can be applied in every situation and achieve universal success.

In fact, no system or organization will win the world for Christ automatically. The unconverted world is not going to get excited about Christian activities as they might do about winning the lottery, because churches work in a different way. Most people have no prior interest in anything that goes on in church. Unsaved folk cannot make head or tale of some church practices if they slip into the back row. The simple teaching of the gospel makes no sense to some until the Holy Spirit twists their minds back into shape.

Common sense is part of the pack of talents that we have received from God and those talents are to be invested. If we have only one talent – or even half a talent – and do not consider ourselves worth very much, we must still give what little we have. All there is of us is needed for all there is of God. We are engaged in the world's most important business. The world uses its intelligence and so should believers. The world has its priorities and interests and believers are under daily pressure to conform. It would be easy to think like the world and accept the world's priorities.

> If we are to do God's work, we must do it and not leave it to means or systems to do it for us.

Without the gospel light, night would fall and the world would revert to pagan barbarism, superstitious fear, and moral confusion. Wherever we see decency, free and happy people with concern and kindness free of corruption and fear, we can be sure that it came from Christianity – from Jesus.

Christ brought us life and immortality. Whatever values have lifted nations came into the world with Christ. Until he conquered death, the grave was a dark place, or at best a twilight zone peopled by the shadows of once living people. The prospect of death was a dark funeral pall hanging over the human race. In this third millennium we are watching the effects of the loss of Christian hope, the only real hope ever known. *"Christ Jesus has destroyed death and has brought life and immortality to light through the gospel"* (2 Timothy 1:10).

There are individuals who do not belong to a church, who do their own thing, "paddling their own canoe" and claiming to go as the Spirit leads. The Holy Spirit does not dart around like a will-o'-the-wisp nor does he prompt erratic action. He is the Spirit of order and faithfulness. We are "workers together." It is a joint operation and no individuals should be hanging loose around the perimeters without God-ordained fellowship or support, doing their own thing. This is not a private war.

When we lay hands on the sick, we are everybody's hands. The gospel preacher stands up with the church behind him, as when Peter stood with the 120 on the day of Pentecost and said, *"We all are witnesses"*, all one in Christ (Acts 2:32). This is God-given unity, the greatest dynamic force on earth. Jesus continues *"all that he began to do"* (Acts 1:1) through his body, the church. Working together is a major means to save some. That is the Biblical pattern, preaching the same word with the same empowering Holy Spirit and with the same signs following, the same results. The "means" most mentioned in the New Testament is cooperation. It is important to *"keep the unity of the Spirit through the bond of peace"* (Ephesians 4:3). When we are born again, we are part of the church, body members; some are hands, some feet, some brains and all of us have a voice, the voice of all fellow-workers (1 Corinthians 12:14-27).

Systems do not bring about revival. Means do not save. The Psalmist hits the nail on the head when he explains why he does not trust in chariots and horses: *"I know that the Lord saves his anointed; he answers him from his holy heaven with the saving power of is right hand"* (Psalm 20:6).

Prayer, our relationship with God, and our obedience are the vital concerns. To save people, each person can do what he or she can, but the work is witness, the same outreach for the lost. God's word has not changed and nothing can be done without people hearing the word.

To sum up, if we are to do God's work, we must **do** it and not leave it to means or systems to do it for us. The latest book can all too easily become the latest fashion. New stresses, variations on teaching appear as "best-sellers" hyped by publishers with an eye for sales opportunities.

The world is still no friend of God. No novelty will cause people to rush to church. Sometimes people talking about opening up the old wells, but why were they closed? Usually they silted up with modern ideas.

Archimedes said, "Give me a lever long enough and a fulcrum on which to place it, and I shall move the world." The church is the fulcrum and the gospel is the lever. Our aim is to put the gospel into every home in the world. I did that in several countries, by distributing **From Minus to Plus** to every household. It was not expected to be a short cut to national revival (as some supposed) but a sincere effort to reach more people with the gospel. The initiative brought many to Christ.

Whatever way we find to do the job or to help those doing it, we must reach the population of 6 billion living on earth, more than all the people that have ever occupied this planet until now. It presents the church with its greatest all-time opportunity. It needs big efforts, enterprise and boldness. To bring the good news to 6 thousand million people involves sacrificing time, financial support, imagination, resourcefulness and dedication. There are at least 600 million born-again Christians – one in ten of the global population. I want to harness this vast force for the glory of God. I want heaven to be excited, rejoicing like never before, at what is happening.

There are now many more ways of "preaching" the gospel to every creature than were available in early Christian times. With modern facilities, present-day believers can reach more people with the gospel than all Christians have reached in 2,000 years. It is very much an end-time situation.

Time is short. We do not have a century or two to win the people who are alive now. Our generation of believers must reach this generation. No one need be idle. Even children can gather a few gleanings. The harvest is ripe but the reapers are few – that is still true today. Now is the day of salvation.

Questions

1. Can you think of things that have changed in the church's approach to evangelism?
2. What role does common sense have to play in our activities?

We know also that the Son of God has come.
He is the true God and eternal life.

1 John 5:20

CHAPTER 7

How did they begin?

*"Set apart for me Barnabas and Saul for the work
to which I have called them."*

Acts 13:2

The first disciples began witnessing with no previous experience, no methods, no techniques, and no seminars to show them how. What was their way?

It began when Jesus, born in Judea, strolled along the beach, chanced upon a group of Galilean lake fishermen, and invited them to go along with him to be fishers of men. From that raw material he made apostles and world-changers, historic figures who will never be forgotten.

When Christ left this earth, the whole future of the faith hung on their shoulders. These were locals who had never traveled farther than their fishing boats could carry them. It is to them, their burning ardor and unflinching sacrifice that we owe our knowledge of salvation. The world, too, owes them an immense debt, the first glimmerings of truly civilized life. They introduced faith, love, hope, forgiveness, gentleness, and values foreign to the ancient culture of the pagan world. The word of God slowly leavened society. Marcus Aurelius, an intellectual and a Stoic, became Roman Emperor in AD 161 and had sayings of Christ inscribed on the walls of Rome.

The first converts were Jews and the first church was in Jerusalem. Thousands came into the faith, many of them temple priests. For some 20 years, even when other Christians were scattered through other places, the apostles themselves remained in Jerusalem, building up their agenda of faith and work. The church centered on the temple (see Acts 6:7, 8:1, 21:20). World vision did not capture them for some years. John wrote *"For God so loved the world"* (John 3:16) but that was later. Jewish believers tended to think of Jesus only as the Messiah for Israel. Even when Jesus rose from the dead, the apostles saw his resurrection only in terms of restoring Israel (Acts 1:6). Jesus laid his hand on the globe itself. He said, *"You will be my witnesses in Jerusalem ... and to the ends of the earth"* (Acts 1:8). The Greek word for "ends" is *eschatos*, which might be translated as the "last place on earth."

Rows and Revivals

To start the gospel moving across the nations, God prepared one man, the apostle Paul. By birth he was a Roman citizen, but he was deeply Jewish, calling himself a *"Hebrew of Hebrews"* (Philippians 3:5). His personal interests were to save his own race (Romans 9:1-4). He settled for a while in Antioch, a Gentile city with a large Jewish population, affording Paul experience of both cultures. God called him to carry the gospel abroad (Acts 13:1) and after some time, with the blessing of the church in Antioch, he set off on his first major journey. Wherever he went during his recorded career, his priority was his own people.

That turned out to be God's way. When he reached a new destination, Paul's method was to visit synagogues first. Jewish synagogues existed throughout the Mediterranean region. Jews who had either been driven abroad or had left on business created colonies in cities throughout the Roman Empire and kept the traditions of Moses. Peter's first epistle is written to Jews *"scattered throughout Pontus, Galatia, Cappadocia, Asia and Bithynia,"* areas of Asia Minor (1 Peter 1:1). Paul himself belonged to the Diaspora. He was born in the Jewish quarter of Tarsus in Cilicia, a sizeable city in the south-eastern corner of what is now Turkey (Acts 22:3).

Hundreds of thousands of Jews had fled their own country, which was so beset by enemy brutalities. After the fall of Assyria and the captivity of Babylon 600 years before Christ, the Jewish remnant faced constant tyranny. A century before Christ Antiochus IV, a Syrian, set out to destroy the religion of the Jews through persecution and slaughter. Victims are mentioned in Hebrews 11. Driven abroad, the dispersed Jews became the channel through which Paul reached the Gentiles.

Paul became a believer in Damascus two or three years after Christ's resurrection and *"at once he began to preach in the synagogues that Jesus is the Son of God"* (Acts 9:20). That was his method. In Jerusalem *"he moved about, speaking boldly in the name of the Lord. He talked and debated with the Grecian Jews"* (Acts 9:28-29). As he moved from one country to another, he would first make contact with people by attending the local synagogue, where, as a Jewish rabbi, he could teach. Usually enemies would stir up opposition and each time he turned to the Gentiles, he triggered any number of rows and revivals.

That is the backdrop against which the pioneers of the gospel worked. It was bold, adventurous work finding a way to reach the world. Paul got in wherever he could, risking humiliation and rejection so that *"by all possible means I might save some"* (1 Corinthians 9:22). Christians were imaginative, venturesome and not tied to any one approach or gimmick. Not only Paul but his converts, too, risked going where they were not sure of being welcome.

Paul spent two years presenting the gospel in the lecture hall of Tyrannus in Ephesus. In Athens he disputed with local Jews, Epicurean and Stoic philosophers and was summoned to the Court of the Areopagus in the Royal Portico. That court had authority in matters of morals and religious ideas. The court was not a large audience, nor was it public, but the apostle presented the claims of Christ without compromise. Some were convinced, including Dionysius, an Areopagite council member. In Rome, Paul preached Christ crucified and did not hesitate to remind people that Rome was guilty of that monstrous crime. Before him, Peter had charged a Jewish multitude with Christ's death. Stephen also spoke fearlessly, pointing out to the religious leaders that they had always resisted the Holy Spirit. He knew he would pay dearly for his unsparing honesty, but the urgency of his message demanded that the risk be taken.

The legend is that the apostles met to decide which country each of them would evangelize. It is fairly sure that Thomas, and perhaps Bartholomew, went to India and died there for the gospel. Those pioneers all exhibited tremendous enterprise and courage. Living today in an age which has been so affected by Christianity, it is hard for us to visualize what it was like then to break into the spiritual and moral darkness when the habits, culture, beliefs and morals of the whole world were godless and largely barbaric, despite the military might and splendors of the Roman Empire.

The Discipleship Agenda

The gospel came in as unobtrusively as an ocean tide. Its pioneers were not only apostles and evangelists but a whole host of ordinary and unknown believers. Half of them were slaves who nonetheless boldly faced the possibility of suffering and even death for Christ. A moving example came to light in excavated Rome. An inscription was found scratched on a kitchen wall lampooning a palace page boy. It showed a crucified man with a donkey's head and the words "Alexamenos worships his God." That young lad had evidently not been afraid to confess and worship Christ in the boys' quarters and to speak of him on the cross. Somebody also scratched on a wall "Alexamenos is faithful," perhaps Alexamenos himself.

Christians never dreamed then of not carrying out Christ's Great Commission. That was what being a Christian meant. It was the discipleship agenda. Until the beginning of the fourth century, AD 313, death was a constant menace for witnesses. However, long before the empire became officially Christian, it was claimed that the towns and markets were filled with believers and the pagan temples deserted.

Young Christians were also ready to die for Christ and would report themselves to the authorities as believers. Their devotion to Jesus Christ was supreme. His peerless greatness blazed through his obscure birth in a cattle shed, his life in a tenth rate eastern town, and his crucifixion as a criminal. He was more than loved; he was worshipped. Jews were brought up in strict understanding of one God who would send someone to Israel – the anointed one. There had never been anyone else like that; no one compared with Jesus. Indeed, there has never been anyone like him since.

> The gospel came in as unobtrusively as an ocean tide. Its pioneers were not only apostles and evangelists but a whole host of ordinary and unknown believers.

Photographed in Color

Christ left no ritual routines as observances by which to acquire salvation and reach heaven for he himself is our salvation. He only asked us to remember him in baptism and in bread and wine. He did not tell us to remember his death but to take bread and wine in remembrance of him (Luke 22:19). When we preach the gospel, Jesus Christ, we must understand whom we are talking about. The name of Jesus is not a talisman, a logo or a formula. We are referring to him – the Christ of the Scriptures and all that he is.

The Old Testament picture is an outline of Jesus; the New Testament photographed him in color. The Old Testament speaks of God and Jesus said it spoke of him. He "fulfilled" the Scriptures – fleshed them out, gave them body and life. Christ is evidence of what the prophets foretold but he was bigger than that. John the Baptist witnessed to him but he saw Jesus grow far beyond his prophecies. *"He must become greater; I must become less,"* he declared (John 3:30).

God testified of himself not just as "God" but gave himself an identity and a name. He first spoke to Moses: *"They will know that I am the Lord their God who brought them out of Egypt"* (Exodus 29:46). That is said 7 times in Exodus. There are many ideas about God but the true God is the God of deliverance. We begin with God the Creator and the God of providence, judgment and holiness, but soon reach the fuller revelation of God the Redeemer, the Healer, the Shepherd, the ever-present One.

John's first epistle describes the great work of Christ delivering the world from wickedness and the devil, and says, *"We know also that the Son of God has come. He is the true God and eternal life"* (1 John 5:20). He is the One who calls us as witnesses. We witness to **that** Christ, the Christ of a thousand glories delineated in the ancient word of God, not a legend, a phantom, a fiction, but the One identified by his matchless and inconceivable greatness.

> God's word is the staff of life. There is no substitute in all creation or in all history. He is the completion of life.

We witness to him because he is what he says he is. He revealed himself to us for our advantage and hope. He made us to know him and he meets our restlessness and longing: *"The desire of all nations will come"* (Haggai 2:7). All people feel the need of him without knowing what it is they lack. The missing piece is Jesus. He meets the groping of our ignorance. Mankind has produced ten thousand creeds and panaceas, but evangelism presents the answer by presenting Jesus. In Athens Paul found an altar to an unknown god and said, *"What you worship as something unknown I am going to proclaim to you"* (Acts 17:23). That is what we do, we proclaim Jesus to people who do not know him. Nothing is ready without him. God said, *"It is not good for the man to be alone"* (Genesis 2:18) and made a wife for Adam. He also said, *"Man does not live on bread alone but on every word that comes from the mouth of the Lord"* (Deuteronomy 8:3). His word is the staff of life. There is no substitute in all creation or in all history. He is the completion of life.

John's Gospel begins majestically: *"In the beginning was the Word."* He uses that name with its awesome meanings about Jesus. To the Greeks the Word was the force or the being beyond everything, holy, unreachable and unknowable. Jews also spoke of the Word, the voice of Yahweh. John tells us that Jesus was all that and more: *"In him was life and that life was the light of men"* (John 1:4), the light of intelligence, self-consciousness and God-consciousness.

The Evangelistic Gospel

The gospel is always evangelistic, intended to be passed on by word of mouth. In the New Testament every word for evangelism is a speech word. The gospel is not a mere theory in a book, a mummified idea, but a living oral proclamation. The gospel is meant to be heard, presented. The word of God is alive. It flows with life. We have the Bible not because it has been preserved as an ancient document. It is not a museum exhibit; it is alive. Living things do not need preserving.

When Paul addressed the Athenians, he "proclaimed" the gospel. For "gospel" Paul used the Greek word *euangelion*, which meant not just news but good news. The English word "gospel" comes from an Anglo Saxon word meaning "good tidings". We are spreading "good news" not "good information." The gospel is always a personal announcement from the mouth of a messenger who has made a glad discovery.

More than that. The good news proclaimed a change in the world's affairs for everybody, tidings of a battle won and a great enemy overthrown. Mark's first verse is *"The beginning of the gospel [euangelion, good news] about Jesus Christ."* He had been pre-empted by an angel at the birth of Jesus: *"I bring you good news of great joy"* (Luke 2:10). He used the same Greek word for "good news" and added another one, the Greek *chara*, "great joy." Paul said he owed a debt to both Jew and Gentile – he knew that they had a right to hear the good news and to experience the joy of knowing Jesus Christ.

Many words are used for the communication of the gospel, such as speaking, talking, announcing, and making known. It is easy to imagine someone whispering the good news to a workmate, almost like a conspirator so that enemies would not hear. Three Greek words are particularly gospel words: *kerygma, euangelizo, martureo;* they mean "proclamation," "to announce good news," and "to testify."

> God wants us involved in his grand scheme. He gives us a uniquely privileged position.

Some modern scholars are always talking about the *kerygma* and what its contents were. It seems to me overwhelmingly obvious that the *kerygma* refers to heralding Jesus Christ – he was the content of the message. Romans 16:25 Paul speaks of *"the proclamation* [kerygma] *of Jesus Christ"*. He was talking about what the gospel is, not the act of preaching. The apostles did not sacrifice everything to preach a joyless doctrine. There are modern scholars who do not seem to realize that whatever the apostles preached was exciting, wonderful, or they would never have traveled so far to say anything. They went out into the world because Jesus and joy were the contents of the *kerygma.* Nobody ever has invented anything like it. It is found in no other religion or philosophy.

The awesome revelation of God in Christ ruptured the eternal heavens but is nothing unless told. God wants us involved in his grand scheme. We may not really understand why God relies on us for this all-important purpose but that is his astounding plan. He gives us a uniquely privileged position.

Euangelion – the gospel – is particularly Paul's word; it occurs in connection with him 56 times out of 76 in the New Testament. It is the good news of everlasting life, resurrection, truth, peace, salvation. Nowadays the word *euangelion* is never used for news about secular events. It has become a Christian word, for the gospel is unique and superlative. No other good news is as good as the gospel.

When John the Baptist preached, he said, *"Repent for the kingdom of heaven is near"* (Matthew 3:2). It sounded more like a warning or threat than something to be joyful about. By contrast, Matthew 4:23 says, *"Jesus went preaching the good news of the kingdom."* John the Baptist did not announce the news as good news but Jesus did. John predicted it but Jesus presented it.

The word *euangelion* is not an announcement or a promise of something to come but a declaration of what has already come. Preaching it does not usher it in or make it happen; it is a fact already. The gospel has this wonderful content: it tells us what God has done. The cross is the one thing that nothing can change. It is more than words, more than a theory, system or doctrine. Jesus really did come to earth, he died and he rose again. Nothing can undo that. It is what the gospel is all about, the rock on which we can safely stand. World commotions, upheavals, changes and wars all beat against that rock; storm winds and roaring seas test its strength but it cannot be shaken.

Modern technology and power can bring the cross into focus but not shift it. *"God ... reconciled us to himself through Christ, not counting men's sins against them"* (2 Corinthians 5:18-19). It is as if he were telling prisoners that the doors to their cells were all unlocked. If they believed it, they could walk out free. As Jesus said to the dead young man at Nain, *"Young man, get up!"* (Luke 7:14). Believers have been given the *"ministry of reconciliation"* and as ambassadors we say, *"Be reconciled to God."* God is reconciled to us however sullen our enmity. (See 2 Corinthians 5:17-20.)

The other well-used word for gospel communication – *martureo*, "to testify" – lies behind the English word "martyr". Christians who have died for Christ are called "martyrs," people who gave their lives for witness and testified to their faith by their sacrifice. Stephen was the first martyr. His death was watched by a young man who probably never got over what he saw – Saul of Tarsus.

John writes about *"the testimony* [marturia] *about God"* (1 John 5:9). In Numbers 17:7 and Exodus 25:22 God is a witness to himself in the Tent of the Testimony and the Ark of the Testimony. Originally, *martureo* was confirmation of an event. It related to memory, speaking about something known directly and personally, especially in a court of law. John uses *martureo* some 43 times in his Gospel and epistles, but never the word *euangelion* or *gospel*. Why? John's Gospel is the gospel of ongoing action and continuing experience. For him witnessing was not occasional but a life-long attitude, our lives a constant reminder or testimony to the truth of Jesus. What Jesus did for believers should mark and distinguish them as Jesus people.

Each of these three important words carries the same thought – that we are what we preach. The messenger is the message. If we preach Christ we are Christians. If we preach the Holy Spirit, we are Spirit-filled. It is God's way today of revealing himself to the world. In us his word is made flesh. All we have to be is what God makes us.

Question

What can you say about the method Paul used to spread the gospel?

CHAPTER 8

Jesus' Casebook

"He is able to save."

Hebrew 7:25

Omnipotence was helpless in the face of human willfulness. Using force was not the answer. In this chapter we shall see the first examples of a different kind of power – the power of salvation.

A man is not a good husband just by flexing his muscles. We could not be saved by brute force. In fact, no one knew what could save us. God committed himself to the task, investing personal effort and sacrifice to the point of shedding blood. *"Without the shedding of blood there is no forgiveness"* (Hebrew 9:22).

God was prepared for that at creation. It meant redemption. Creation was not cheap. A word made the world but it later cost him blood, sweat and tears. The 6 days making everything in creation culminated in 6 hours on a cross. *"The Lamb was slain from the creation of the world"* (Revelation 13:8). Salvation is the artery through which the life-giving blood of the whole Bible flows. When God made trees, he made one for his cross.

After creation, the Bible describes the Flood. We read that *"the earth was corrupt and full of violence"* (Genesis 6:11); the ground had been defiled by all the blood shed in acts of violence and anger. When Cain murdered Abel, God said that the blood cried out from the ground (Genesis 4:10). Similarly in Hosea 6:8, God declared that Gilead was *"stained with footprints of blood"* and Psalm 106:38 reminds us that *"the land was desecrated by blood."*

The violence was an issue of such provocation that God caused a great flood to bring it to an end. Afterwards he said to Noah,

"Whoever sheds the blood of man, by man shall his blood be shed"
(Genesis 9:6). Murder must be met by judgment; blood must cover blood. God gave that law because the waters of the deluge had not cleansed the bloodstained earth. Among Moses' altar offerings there was no offering for murder – no forgiveness. No animal blood was enough to cover the war and bloodshed of centuries. Jesus said, *"This generation will be held responsible for the blood of all the prophets that has been shed since the beginning of the world"* (Luke 11:50). More than human blood was needed to put things right. Only the sacrificial blood of the Lamb of God could cover over the blood of violence. God had appointed a day of atonement which involved shedding *"his own blood"* (Acts 20:28). *"The blood of Jesus, God's son, purifies us from all sin"* (1 John 1:7).

Mercy Descending

The mercy of God that came to earth with Jesus is so well known to us that we only half appreciate it. We have a clear example of God's mercy in the conversion of Saul of Tarsus. He, who became Paul the apostle, had a tremendous sense of it, saying, *"The grace of our Lord was poured out on me abundantly, along with the faith and love that are in Christ Jesus."* He was talking about his personal experience but he added, *"Here is a trustworthy saying that deserves full acceptance: Christ Jesus came into the world to save sinners – of whom I am the worst"* (1 Timothy 1:14-15). In other words, his experience could be that of others, too. Some 600 years before Christ, the prophet Ezekiel was sent to announce *"A ruin! A ruin! I will make it a ruin!"* and Isaiah, one of the greatest prophets, was sent to *"make the heart of this people calloused. Otherwise they might see with their eyes, hear with their ears, understand with their hearts, and turn and be healed."* This was to go on *"until the cities lie ruined and the land is utterly forsaken"* (Ezekiel 21:27, Isaiah 6:10-12). God sent Jeremiah with a similarly depressing message: *"Today I appoint you over nations and kingdoms to uproot and tear down, to destroy and overthrow, to build and to plant!"* (Jeremiah 1:10).

One thing rarely mentioned but very startling is that until Christ came the only record of the lost being found involved King Saul's donkeys (1 Samuel 9:20). In the work of Jesus,

> Salvation is the artery through which the life-giving blood of the whole Bible flows.

God demonstrated his authority and power to save. Jesus declared that he was the true shepherd and that all those who had preceded him were thieves and robbers; he had come *"to seek and to save what was lost"* (Luke 19:10).

The first examples of redemption are found in the gospels. Full of grace and truth, Jesus' treatment of certain individuals demonstrated God's saving power and will, reclaiming people who were beyond the pale, social derelicts.

There is an enigmatic Scripture in Matthew 11:12. Jesus said, *"The kingdom of God has been forcefully advancing and forceful men lay hold of it."* It is his anticipation of multitudes storming the kingdom. Christ gave his apostle Peter the gospel keys to open the gates. Thousands at once emigrated to the kingdom of God, leaving the power of Satan behind. On that day, the first day of Pentecost, the never-ending stream of souls into the kingdom began. The kingdom was taken by the "force" of faith.

Blessing Rank Sinners

The first people to enter the kingdom were those called by Jesus himself. The first instances of individuals receiving salvation directly from Christ are an education for us in our work of witness and evangelism and we must make space here to consider two or three of them.

Actually, the first were Andrew and (we think) John, who got Peter. The next day Jesus called Philip, and Philip brought Nathanael. Jesus said that God had given them to him (John 10:29, 17:9,24). Theologians puzzle over this as we do not read that they were ever convicted of sin or repented. However, they exhibited faith, trusting so implicitly and following Jesus when they knew so little about him or even who he was. He was still an unknown. Jesus appears to have saved them by his own sovereign inclination but, then, he did know what was in people (John 2:25).

That is still true today. Evangelism often insists that converts follow the classical pattern. However, there may be no outward sign of conversion. The fact is that Jesus knew and God knows what goes on in the depths of a human soul and personality. He cannot be hoodwinked by any pretensions, any mere show of conversion. He reads the hearts of all. If there was any anguish over sin and deep contrition in Samaria following Philip's proclamation of the gospel, we have no record of it. However, there was *"great joy in that city"* over the work of the Holy Spirit and soon after the evidence of genuine salvation was given because the people received the Holy Spirit and spoke in tongues (Acts 8).

Jesus said, *"If I drive out demons by the finger of God, then the kingdom of God has come to you"* (Luke 11:20). The sign of the kingdom was his power to drive out unclean spirits, but far greater was his power to save.

Jesus shocked religious leaders when he blessed rank sinners. They considered sinners to be cursed, ignorant of Moses' law and religious traditions, but Jesus befriended them. He said, *"The good news is preached to the poor"* (Matthew 11:5). That was a revolution. To the religious perfectionists the poor were untouchable, but Jesus preached to them, loved them, forgave them and healed them.

The greatest stir was caused by Jesus' dealings with the taxman called Zacchaeus, a heartless character prepared to sell his soul for money. He was a lackey of Rome, the occupying power, and nobody wanted anything to do with him. He had caged himself behind bars of gold. When he heard about Jesus, he ventured out to see him as he passed along the road. When the crowd caught sight of the hated taxman, they were determined not to let him through and pushed him around, making it clear that he was not wanted. So casting dignity aside, Zacchaeus clambered monkey-like into a sycamore tree, from where he was sure to see this man who was the talk of the town. Of course, his chosen perch only made him more conspicuous. Bystanders probably pointed at him and laughed. Then Jesus came by, saw him and told him to come down quickly.

Evangelism Justified

Zacchaeus could hardly believe what happened next. Christ asked him for hospitality and Zacchaeus *"came down at once"* (Luke 19:6). That was an evening that Zacchaeus would never forget; he and Jesus looked at another across the supper table.

Zacchaeus was a calculating character but had not reckoned on dealing with anybody like Jesus; he had never imagined a man like that. He felt as if his inner self was exposed to the most genial judge in the world. Jesus felt sorry for him – loved him. His shrunken soul began expanding like a sponge soaking up water. Then a thought stole into his mind that had never occurred to him before, the idea of giving money to the poor. Jesus saw it and said, *"Today salvation has come to this house"* (Luke 19:9). That was a taste of things to come.

Saving this rogue had a cost for Jesus – his reputation. Zacchaeus worked for the occupying power of hated Rome and the people saw Jesus befriend him. It did damage to Jesus' popularity. His foes would make much of it. His reply may have cut little ice with those impervious critics but it uncovered the truth about the character of Jesus: *"The Son of Man came to seek and to save what was lost."* That sums up Jesus, our Lord. If it sums up any of us, it simply shows that we are following his example. It is not reputation we seek, but renewed lives.

> It is not reputation
> we seek,
> but renewed lives.

No one had ever known personal spiritual conversion before. Christ's visit to Zacchaeus proved it possible. Prophets had called for it but never seen it. Isaiah's prompting, for example, was *"Let the wicked forsake his way and the evil man his thoughts. Let him turn to the Lord, and he will have mercy on him, and to our God, for he will freely pardon"* (Isaiah 55:7). However, the wicked did not forsake his way. Such things did not happen then.

We know what normal people were like in those days from Psalms written for public use. They did not hide their feelings and never called on God to save the wicked; instead, they openly appealed to God to rend the heavens and destroy them. God did rend the heavens but Jesus came down – and destroyed nobody. John the Baptist, the last of the old-time prophets, expected the same thing to happen, but Jesus said, *"The Son of Man did not come to destroy men's lives, but to save them"* (Luke 9:56). This was not the deliverance that the Palmists meant! Jesus carried no sword. On the cross he himself bore the very judgment that they wanted to be pronounced on sinners.

Salvation is Spiritual and Physical

Another account of Jesus' work of salvation is found in Mark 2:1-12 and Luke 5:17-26, from which we can draw a great deal of encouragement. Jesus was staying at a house in Capernaum – perhaps his own. He had attracted the attention of religious leaders, Pharisees and doctors of law, from many towns including Jerusalem – possibly sent to investigate him on behalf of the religious authorities. The house was jam-packed with people.

Four men turned up carrying a paralyzed man on a stretcher but could not get to Jesus because of the crowd. However, it was an eastern house with a flat roof and an outside staircase. Determined not to be put off and full of faith for a miracle, they carried the paralytic on to the roof, which was only made of wooden slats, straw and branches, over the open yard where Jesus was speaking. They pulled away the light roofing and deposited their friend literally at Christ's feet – without an apology. The scene highlights the eager faith of the four men. We read that *"Jesus saw their faith"* (Mark 2:5). I expect everybody did, and I wonder what the religionists thought of such simple expectant trust.

When Jesus saw **their** faith, he responded by saying to the paralytic, *"Your sins are forgiven."* How could Jesus forgive his sins because of his friends' faith? Sin and sickness were firmly linked in everyone's minds at that time – as were forgiveness and healing – so to see him healed proved to the onlookers that he was forgiven. With his sin wiped out, he got up and walked away. *"The prayer offered in faith will make the sick person well; the Lord will raise him up. If he has sinned, he will be forgiven"* (James 5:15). If Jesus could really forgive, then healing would follow. However, no one expected any such miracle and they challenged Christ's power to forgive.

Jesus asked whether it was easier to say *"Your sins are forgiven"* or to say *"Get up and walk."* Obviously anyone could use the words *"You are forgiven,"* so he explained the extent of his power: *"That you may know that the Son of Man has authority on earth to forgive sins ... He said to the paralyzed man, 'I tell you, get up, take your mat and go home'"* (Luke 5:22-24).

> On that day, the first day of Pentecost, the never-ending stream of souls into the kingdom began. The kingdom was taken by the "force" of faith.

Forgiveness is not the big book in heaven being wiped clean; it is we who are cleansed – in body, soul and mind. Our consciousness is given a spring clean that lasts. Jesus forgives people on earth their sins – with physical effects.

In other words, salvation is not merely spiritual; it is both spiritual and physical. The Old Testament hammers away at that message. God made heaven and earth. He has not withdrawn his interest from the physical and material world that he created. *"God so loved the world ..."* (John 3:16). The earth is as much a sphere of his interest and operations as heaven is. We are to pray, *"Your will be done on earth as it is in heaven"* (Matthew 6:10). That covers miracles and divine providence. Just as he makes a perfect heaven, he wants a perfect earth.

A chapter like Deuteronomy 28 states the truth about the world in which we live. It tells us that to obey God will bring "blessing" in everything we have or do. Psalm 1:3 says, *"Whatever he does prospers."* The theology is wonderful and sound. God founded the world on goodness. God is good. *"God saw all that he had made, and it was very good"* (Genesis 1:31). Sin and disobedience disturb the natural order of things. Faith restores it, puts the disjointed parts back together in our lives.

> Forgiveness is not the big book in heaven being wiped clean; it is we who are cleansed – in body, soul and mind. Our consciousness is given a spring clean that lasts. Jesus forgives people on earth their sins – with physical effects.

That belief underlies the whole of the Old Testament. God did not make his appearance in nature because of a special covenant, a special arrangement with Israel, but as fact, the way the world is made. The Creator never surrendered his rights over his creation.

Gospel truth is in harmony and agreement with the truth of creation. It is the God of creation who saves us because we are part of creation. He makes no distinctions between nature and spirit. He saves us where we are and as we are, covering the whole scene. The word of the gospel is physical-spiritual power. Unbelief shuts the door on God. Jesus saves people, people with feelings, physical and psychological beings. He saves human beings made of flesh and blood, not ghosts.

Response from God

Luke 5:17 tells us that where the miracle healing of the paralyzed man took place, *"the power of the Lord was present for him to heal the sick."* It is tragic that the only person healed had to be let in through the roof; as far as we know, no one else was healed even though the house was full to overflowing of people, no doubt most of them sick. The religionists were there but Jesus did nothing for them, neither cleansing nor healing.

Some churches are in that sorry state. People come to worship God as if he just sat on the throne listening to the prayers and songs with a benign smile on his face. Nothing is expected to happen except in some vague spiritual sense that the singing and praying will supposedly do the people good. I hope it does, but where is the response from God? The routine goes on week in, week out; nothing happens and nothing is preached for things to happen. Jesus is an invited guest, kept at a polite and formal distance, in a spiritual dimension and not in the real world. A manifestation of his presence would be too likely to disrupt dignity and order. The paralyzed man's four friends came to a gathering of listeners just like that and ripped the roof off. That is typical of New Testament Christian faith. It is dynamic – it takes the roof off!

A further illustration of salvation is given us in Luke 7:36-50, where we are told about a woman who had lived a sinful life in that town and was so notorious that even Pharisees knew her. (I wonder how they did!) The story emphasizes that to religious people the woman was odious, not fit to touch.

As was customary in those parts, the dinner guests were reclining at the table. They had no chairs, so they were half sitting on rugs, propping themselves up with their left arm and using their right hand for the food, their bare feet stretched out behind them. The table had probably been set in the warm sunshine in the open courtyard of the house, where there was more room.

The woman was not prevented from entering the house – perhaps it was a social custom to let passers-by in. Standing behind Jesus as he reclined, she poured perfume on his head and feet and wept, her tears wetting his feet. Her mascara ran down her face and black drops landed on Jesus' feet. She was worried that she had defiled him so she fell to her knees, bent over, let down her tresses, and tried to wipe the tears away. Then she kissed his feet over and over again.

> The Creator never surrendered his rights over his creation. Gospel truth is in harmony and agreement with the truth of creation.

What a scene! What love! We are talking about salvation. That is what it is like, not a theory frozen in a theological textbook. How many churches today would accommodate such passionate worship? Yet there she is in the Bible – an example of what it means to be forgiven. That woman knew that she had been forgiven. She would appear to have met Christ somewhere previously and that was where it had happened. She felt clean in a powerful way and took the opportunity to thank Jesus. Her personality was transformed. That is salvation.

The first Europeans to hear the gospel were the members of Cornelius' household in Caesarea. Jesus continued to do what he had started and the conversion of Cornelius was so typical of him, though now it took place through an apostle. Peter had the keys of the kingdom. That is, his privilege was to be the first man in the Christian age to pass on the gospel. In this instance he was God-directed to non-Jews, Gentiles, though against his own instincts. The sermon that he preached in Pisidian Antioch was simply about Jesus. The heart of his message was *"Through Jesus the forgiveness of sins is proclaimed to you"* (Acts 13:38). His words were the heart of the gospel and the effect was electric. God broke through into the world outside Israel. Everyone was filled with the Holy Spirit and began to speak in tongues, the clear evidence of the God who made man's body and spirit.

Our preaching will always be in power and demonstration as long as we preach Jesus in faith and expectation, having been anointed with the Holy Spirit.

A common criticism of evangelists is that they should "make disciples," but they cannot produce instant spiritu-

> A common criticism of evangelists is that they should "make disciples," but they cannot produce instant spiritual adults.

al adults. Jesus did not make everyone that heard him a disciple either. He worked on some of them to turn them into disciples. However, a lot of people loved him. Making disciples of converts is the work of the church. The woman who kissed the feet of Jesus was not a disciple in the strictest sense of the word, but having been forgiven much, Jesus said, she loved much, and love is everything.

Questions

1. Is there any place for force in Christian work?
2. What does Jesus show us about forgiveness?

Some wandered in desert wastelands,
finding no way to a city where they could settle.
They were hungry and thirsty and their lives ebbed away.
Then they cried out to the Lord in their trouble
and he delivered them from their distress.
He led them by a straight way to a city
where they could settle.

Psalm 107:4-7

CHAPTER 9

The Combination Lock of Salvation

"I will give you the keys of the kingdom of heaven."
Matthew 16:19

To obtain a cup of cold water, just turn on the tap. It is wonderful stuff. Life without water is impossible. Only God could invent it and God is the sole supplier. He pours out millions of tons daily from the heavens.

Salvation is the same. We can tap into it any time, but it is totally God's work. Life, the kind of life God intended his creatures to enjoy, is impossible without the salvation of our God. *"I, even I, am the Lord, and apart from me there is no savior"* (Isaiah 43:11).

It is all of God, yet we are needed to take it to the world. God planted Eden, but Adam had to tend it. We can take the waters of salvation to the thirsty. *"The Spirit and the bride say 'Come!' And let him who hears say, 'Come!' Whoever is thirsty, let him come, and whoever wishes, let him take the free gift of the water of life"* (Revelation 22:17). Where salvation is not preached, nobody is saved. The cup of the water of life must be put to the lips of a thirsty world. That is our work, and that is something we can all do. That is why we are here. *"With joy you will draw water from the wells of salvation"* (Isaiah 12:3).

When Jesus walked on earth, he exercised his authority to save. Disciples simply came to him and he sealed them to himself for ever. In his prayer before his arrest, he said, *"You granted him authority over all people that he might give eternal life to all those you have given him"* (John 17:2). That is who he is. The Gospels show the Savior at work saving people. He walked along the beach where a few young fishing men were busy with their nets and invited them to follow him. They did so. Then he saw Levi sitting at the tax collector's booth and said, *"Follow me!"* Levi shut his desk and followed Jesus. All who came to Jesus were accepted and received salvation, although none of them underwent a classical evangelical conversion. It is not what we do that matters. It is Jesus who saves.

In his prayer before his death Jesus confirmed that those same men and women who had simply followed him belonged to God. *"Father, you granted him authority over all people that he might give eternal life to all those you have given him. Now this is eternal life: that they may know you, the only true God, and Jesus Christ, whom you have sent"* (John 17:2-3). Anyone may come to him. If they do, God has called them, although *"many are invited but few are chosen"* (Matthew 22:14).

When I look out at the multitudes attending our gospel campaigns, I realize how different people are from one another, human distinctions being the greatest of all differences. Each of us is a unique universe; there are no clones and no repeats. God alone knows our true nature and name with our personal make-up of tastes, attitudes, desires and reactions. How can I preach and cater for such a mass of different personalities? The gospel solves the problem. Just as everyone needs water, everyone needs the gospel – whether they are prince or pauper, proud or shamed, wise or stupid. The full gospel message is a brimming cup of the water of life.

God deals with Individuals

God's dealings are with individuals, beginning with Adam and with Eve. *"He calls his own sheep by name"* (John 10:3). My campaigns have routine organizational structures built in to care for those turning to Christ but the Lord looks on each one of them as special. Each has his or her own testimony and experience. Our contact with the Lord must be personal. There are no in-betweens. God does not save wholesale, en masse, but always individually. Jesus rose from the dead and the first thing he said was, "Mary!"

and then, "Tell Peter." Peter and Paul enjoyed the same salvation but each conversion was different and unique. Mary Magdalene had 7 demons cast out of her, while the woman at the well asked Jesus for his gift of a well of water. Whatever the circumstances and calling, there is one common experience; each person is saved by knowing Jesus. There is obviously no salvation without Christ because salvation is a Christian idea. Salvation in Christ is atonement, resurrection power and forgiveness. To say one religion is as good as another is meaningless. The question is good for what?

I wondered how God dealt with different people, saving them, before Christ came, that is before the day of salvation, and whether he did. I can recall two special instances, repentant King Manasseh and King David.

The name "Manasseh" is a synonym for wickedness in the book of Kings and for repentance in Chronicles. It has been suggested that his name was Moses but for shame the Hebrew was altered to Manasseh. An open pagan, he even sacrificed his own children in the fires of his gods. He became a prisoner of war and languished in irons for many years, with a hook through his nose. When he turned to God, the Lord received him, an example of supreme wickedness becoming an example of grace. The Prayer of Manasseh, found in the Apocrypha, is not original but sounds as we might imagine a repentant would pray.

The other example is King David, a greatly gifted and complex character. He perpetrated murder and adultery and admitted his guilt. Set above the law as an absolute monarch, he pushed his personal integrity aside to indulge his craving for the beautiful Bathsheba. She became pregnant and to disguise his paternity David ordered her husband Uriah back from battle to spend a night with her. However, out of loyalty to his men who were camping out at the battle front, Uriah declined the opportunity. Failing in this deceit, David ordered Uriah to be placed in battle where he was bound to be killed. His death was reported soon after. David supported a prophet, Nathan, who went to David and challenged the king by denouncing his murderous betrayal of a great soldier.

I have chosen that story as it presents several key salvation words.

Repentance

David repented. In those days, no other king would have considered that there was anything wrong with what David did. His depths of repentance related to his acknowledgment of God. *"Against, you, you only, have I sinned and done what is evil in your sight"* (Psalm 51:4).

God changes attitudes. In the book of Leviticus, God says *"I am the Lord"* 46 times. It is his sole reason for anything and everything. God is the ultimate law, purpose and reason. He does not need to explain why we should do this or that; he simply says *"I am the Lord,"* pointing to the authority behind all the commands: *"Keep my commands and follow them. I am the Lord"* (Leviticus 22:31). Modern life has no basis for its morals other than what it thinks might be relatively best but Israel was far ahead of modern thought. Israel had an absolute raison d'être for daily conduct, the Lord – a thousand years before the rest of the world had even begun to crawl out of ignorance and barbarity. We have not crawled too far even now, especially not where there is a sign saying "God not admitted!"

Few possessed David's understanding, even in Israel in those days. Murder was unforgivable and no atonement or sacrifice existed; death was the only response. Bathsheba's child became sick and David recognized that God was in it. He sought the Lord, fasting and neither washing nor changing his clothes until angels took the child away. The loss brought David's repentance to its peak. He bowed to the will of God, saw himself as bearing the natural consequences of his folly. Yet, at the same time, he knew that God had truly forgiven him.

We are not told that David's great sin came from satanic engineering. David put it down to his own nature. David, who was perhaps vulnerable in his relationship with women, admitted, *"Surely I was sinful at birth, sinful from the time my mother conceived me"* (Psalm 51:5). No doubt Satan was delighted over David's sin but we read in James that *"each one is tempted when, by his own evil desire, he is dragged away and enticed"* (James 1:14). Satan is not omnipresent. He can present himself personally to us one at a time. More than once he turned his attention on David. In 1 Chronicles 21:1, for example, we read that *"Satan rose up against Israel and incited David to take a census of Israel."*

Repentance is the watershed word. Raindrops on the Rocky Mountains fall together but some flow east to the Atlantic and others west to the Pacific oceans.

What kind of repentance is meant? Many criminals "repent" when they are sitting in jail, but it is regret only, brought on by the penalty of their crime. True repentance is a Holy Spirit work, impressing or convincing someone of their evil: *"When he* [the Spirit] *comes he will convict the world of guilt in regard to sin and righteousness and judgment"* (John 16:8). The apostle Peter first saw repentance on the day of Pentecost because the Holy Spirit had begun his work; he said, *"God exalted him (Jesus) to his own right hand as Prince and Savior that he might give repentance and forgiveness of sins to Israel"* (Acts 5:31).

Repentance should not be preached as a threat but as a gift. Jesus said, *"Repentance and forgiveness of sins will be preached in his name to all nations"* (Luke 24:47). It represents the complete turnaround that so many people wish for but lack the strength to begin. The gospel creates the desire for a good life, the will to perform and the power to change. In Christ people can repent; without the Spirit they cannot. That is why our preaching must be in the Spirit. He is the effective element. Our words may be logical but the Spirit plants reasons in the heart.

Grace

The child of David's adultery became ill soon after birth and David prayed for its recovery in the firm belief that God might be gracious. The child actually died, but David did not say, "God was not gracious." He knew God always is. That was one of the specific truths David bequeathed us in the Psalms. For this child only, God's will was not for it to survive. God is full of grace, even when sadness afflicts us. David was not testing God's grace, only whether it applied to this child conceived in sin. He himself was the real case for grace. He trusted the grace of God to forgive him and God did. It does not matter whether God will agree to do everything we think about. Salvation is the one thing – the only thing – that matters and about which we can be totally sure. Whether he answers our private requests or not is no evidence about his grace in salvation.

Flowers lift their heads when the sun shines, and God is our sun. Jesus raised a young man from the dead with the words *"Young man, get up!"*

Here are more keys to the combination lock of salvation. Let's start with 2 Samuel 12:20: *"Then David got up from the ground. After he had washed, put on lotions and changed his clothes, he went into the house of the Lord and worshipped."* David got up from the ground. Everything to do with God is "up." We lift our heads and hearts to him. The command is "Lift up your heads!" not "Hang your heads in shame." Flowers lift their heads when the sun shines, and God is our sun. Jesus raised a young man from the dead with the words *"Young man, get up!"* (Luke 7:14) and the daughter of Jairus saying, *"My child, get up!"* (Luke 8:50). Peter restored Tabitha with similar words: *"Tabitha, get up! She opened her eyes and sat up"* (Acts 9:40). Hearing the gospel, people get up, sit up and stand up. It lifts the fallen, lifts people's spirits, lifts the economy of nations, elevates the poor and cheers the downcast.

Nobody is depressed by the gospel unless blinded by prejudice like the crazed German philosopher Friedrich Nietzsche, who hated Christianity precisely because it inspired revolt. He argued for the "will to power" of the "overman," a superior class of men who mastered others and subdued them, ideas adopted by Adolf Hitler. Christianity infuriated him because it inspired ordinary people to stand up, to be free, confident in God and slaves to nobody. The gospel is far, far beyond a nice church feeling. It is the dynamic behind the universe investing our lives with resurrection energy. Yes! It is "up" for everyone who receives the gospel.

David had fallen as low as anyone could get, even as king, but his insight into God's mercy enabled him to *"get up from the ground"* and back on the throne. Conversion raises us off the ground, unties the leash of earthbound limits, the common lot of people with no God, no heaven and no future. The Lord *"raises the poor from the dust and lifts the needy from the ash heap; he seats them with princes"* (Psalm 113:7). Behind the gospel is the principle of growth, development, increase and improvement.

The evangelist is not a depressor but an uplifter; he does not condemn but delivers from condemnation. He wears a garment of praise and joy, not of sackcloth. He releases rather than binds and brings light, not gloom and doom. He lifts life's heaviness and does not impose a burden.

Health and Freshness

David washed. While he was on the ground, he never changed his clothes. For David, murder clung to him like blood on the hands of Lady Macbeth. He said, *"Wash away all my iniquity. Create in me a pure heart, O God, and renew a steadfast spirit within me"* (Psalm 51:2,10). David washed, freed himself from the dragging load on his conscience; he was washing off the past, the clutter and clinging failures, the hang-ups and regrets. In our age of virus and antibiotics cleansing is more than skin deep, it is clinical.

It is health. Clinical cleansing means the removal of all bacteria. Cleansing by the blood of Christ not only removes every molecule that offends the holiness of God and to which he is sensitive, washing away all that is foul and objectionable, but everything evil to which we ourselves are sensitive. Washing leads to acceptance with God and we can accept ourselves. He forgives us and we can live with ourselves. His blood atones, reconciles and imparts forgiveness.

Washing means welcome! In Victorian England the poor were "the great unwashed," not welcome in the proud chapels and churches. Separate mission halls were opened up for them, but God did not mind their soap-less state. Those mission halls sometimes became like extensions of heaven.

Washing in the blood of Christ is the key to the door, to the blessing of God, the passport into the kingdom of God, and the password into the divine throne-room itself. Heaven is populated by those who have been redeemed by the blood of Christ. In Revelation John saw they had *"washed their robes, and made them white in the blood of the Lamb"* (7:14). Tens of thousands of voices joined together in praise, singing *"Worthy is the Lamb that was slain"* (5:11). The heavenly music was not set in a minor key and all the choir members had washed and were without a stain on their conscience. The tempting devil had been snatched off their shoulder. They sang and sang, free from the dragging sinfulness of the past. They were washed and welcome!

Fragrance

"David put on lotions." The Hebrew word that is used is the same as "anoint", a key word for today. Anointing means not only efficiency and authority, but also beauty. In David's world no man was fit for company until he had poured oils on his head and massaged unguents into the skin, making his face shine. Cosmetics were not just for women; in fact, they were an important feature

of life. Jesus reminded his host that he had failed to provide oils for his head (Luke 7:46). David's original anointing was as king. Without oil he was unkingly, but now, forgiven and restored, he put lotion on his face to shine in renewed majesty.

I proclaim full salvation to include anointing. It is not an optional extra, a luxury, but the mark of reality as opposed to religious theory. John told believers that they bore the royal anointing: *"You have an anointing from the Holy One,"* and *"the anointing you have received from him remains in you"* (1 John 2:20,27). Different kinds of anointing oil contained various ingredients. Oils used in temple anointings had sacred ingredients that were not intended for common use so that a king, priest, or high priest would be recognized by his fragrance.

Our ideal is the unmistakable presence of the Holy Spirit. No ugliness, no dowdiness can be attributed to God. Color not chaos is identified with God – his glory is not mud even though he makes man from mud. The skies are a canvas across which God paints all his dawns and sunsets with no palette other than the dust swept into the cloud by the wind – beauty replacing ashes. He fills emptiness and gives shape to the formless. He himself is the fountain of all color, glory and loveliness. *"May the beauty of the Lord our God rest upon us"* (Psalm 90:17).

> Worship is the greatest act of the human spirit, the unique instinct unlike any other form of life. With worship we operate at the full human level and become more than human, truly the children of God.

Holy purity, the grace of the Spirit's anointing, is spiritual "perfume" making the good lovely and the godly attractive. Jesus was delightful to know: *"All were amazed at the gracious words that came from his lips"* (Luke 4:22). Are we?

Fashion

"David changed his clothes." Down the ages fashion has always decreed the livery of poverty for the poor and penalties if they dressed as the rich. In Israel the High Priest's garments were more than distinguished, they were for God alone to see. Jacob's son Joseph was given a coat of many colors as a sign of his father's favor. God had chosen David to be king with the privilege of royal attire. Falling into a cheap and common sin, he was humiliated, on the ground in unwashed clothing, like any beggar. To regain his anointed and kingly status he changed his clothes, putting on regal attire.

That takes us straight to Colossians. The children of God should be recognizable, putting off *"anger, rage, malice, slander and filthy language."* Instead, we are told, *"Clothe yourselves with compassion, kindness, humility, gentleness and patience. Over all these virtues put on love"* (Colossians 3:8,12,14). Like the Colossians, the Ephesians were also told to *"put on the new self"* (Ephesians 4:24).

A converted man *"clothes himself with Christ"* (Galatians 3:27) and does the world a great favor. Even the world has a secret wish for Christ to come back. He is the one person most people would be glad to meet, but they never will unless they meet him in his people. We follow only one fashion – Christ. We do not invent our own morality and goodness. He is the perfection; the opportunity to put on his habits, his love, his integrity, and his kindness is the offer made to us when we are invited to "clothe ourselves with Christ."

There are changes that we can make. We talk of people "putting on" airs and graces when they speak in a false, supposedly elegant way. That is not what we are talking about: Christ is our role model. We cannot put on Christ and do it falsely. It is a betrayal of an unsuspecting world to put on a cloak of godliness and remain proud and selfish in heart.

Jesus was not a showman; he did not exercise authority and power in an arrogant display of self-love. A mark of all his miracles was his quiet, unpretentious manner. He was astonishing. He could say, *"I am gentle and humble in heart"* (Matthew 11:29) without boasting because he really was like that. He adopted no authoritative stance to cast out demons or heal the sick; *"he drove out the spirits with a word"* (Matthew 8:16). To do his works we need his manner; we need to "put on" the gentleness and humility of our Savior and Lord. This is not just about fashion. What kind of clothing people find attractive can vary from one generation to the next. The Lord has something far better to offer: *"Your beauty should be that of a gentle and quiet spirit, which is of great worth in God's sight"* (1 Peter 3:4).

Direction

David *"went into the house of the Lord and worshipped."* David knew where to go. Without God, life staggers around in a pathless wilderness. We may try to make our own way, laying down a path, but without a goal. The effect of godlessness is expressed in the poetry of Psalm 107:4-7: *"Some wandered in desert wastelands, finding no way to a city where they could settle. They were hungry and thirsty and their lives ebbed away. Then they cried out to the Lord in their trouble and he delivered them from their distress. He led them by a straight way to a city where they could settle."* David was a genius but without the saving grace of God, life collapses for lack of purpose. It gets nowhere because the godless have nowhere they can think of going.

> Repentance should not be preached as a threat but as a gift.

The lowliest worshipper has permanent significance. Who else has? Worship is the greatest act of the human spirit, the unique instinct unlike any other form of life. With worship we operate at the full human level and become more than human, truly the children of God.

David getting up from the ground is a picture of our entire evangelistic purpose. We are not recruiting church members, not signing up adherents. We are saving souls, lifting the multitudes who are weighed down by their past, living in fear and self-condemnation. We bring them in for the anointing of God, and invite them to sit at Jesus' feet *"dressed and in their right mind."* All the gold in the Rand and the rubies in Burma are nothing compared to the value of one soul. We are going out side by side with the great Shepherd, seeking that which was lost.

Questions

1. What part does repentance have to play in
   Christian conversion?
2. David did not get the answer to his prayer that he had hoped for.
   What was his attitude towards God?

CHAPTER 10

Getting Going

"These Jesus sent out with the following instructions:
'As you go ...'"
Matthew 10:5

The Principal of Going

If we want to go somewhere, we first need to start. God does not start us, he does not turn the ignition key. We are either self-starters or we do not start at all. That is one of the core principles that we will be examining in this chapter.

If you need to be pushed, God will not push you. He will lift you out of a pit but not out of an armchair. God wants goers, not sitters. We work and he directs us. If we go, he goes. We speak and he gives us utterance. If you are pushy, push for God and he will get you there. That is what God wants, people with enterprise and vision.

If we sit waiting for the Lord to take the first step, we will sit around for ever. People talk about waiting on the Lord to know his will. His will is for them to be up and doing. It is more comfortable on one's knees than on one's feet but *"how beautiful are the feet of those who bring good news"* (Isaiah 52:7, Romans 10:15).

Paul found one or two converts doing nothing but waiting for Jesus to come back, but that was not the idea of the Christian faith. He said, *"Keep away from every brother who is idle. They are not busy; they are busybodies. Such people we command and urge in the Lord Jesus Christ to settle down and earn the bread they eat. Never tire of doing what is right"* (2 Thessalonians 3:6,11-13).

The initiative to serve God lies with us. For motivation, stimulation, and encouragement open the Bible. It is your mentor. God does not coerce us. He is not a recruiting officer. If we are sluggish, then only we can do anything about it. Jesus wept over Jerusalem saying, *"You were not willing."* They had had abundant cause to seek and serve the Lord but he was not going to force them, although he knew how terrible the consequences would be if they did not. They were a fruitless vine despite all the divine husbandry.

One man, in John 5, had done nothing for 38 years but sit and hope somebody would do something for him, put him into the healing waters and bring him healing. Jesus simply told him to get up, pick up his mat and walk. He could have sat there another few decades or more unless he had done what Jesus said. In John 9 Jesus told a blind man to go and wash in the Pool of Siloam. The gospel puts it like this: *"He went and washed, and came home seeing"* (9:7). He was not healed until he acted and he obviously acted in faith. John's Gospel likes that sort of language. In grammatical terms he uses the participle to show ongoing action John never talks about faith but always about "believing." Christianity is not a plastic, static institution. It is a tree bursting with life; the tree is not dead and its leaves are green, rustling in the breeze.

> If you need
> to be pushed,
> God will not push you.
> He will lift you
> out of a pit but not
> out of an armchair.
> God wants goers,
> not sitters.

When God delivered Israel from Egypt, he told them to have a meal of roast lamb and said, *"This is how you are to eat it: with your cloak tucked into your belt, your sandals on your feet and your staff in your hand. Eat it in haste"* (Exodus 12:11). Ephesians 6:14-15 echoes the same lively spirit: *"Stand firm then, with the belt of truth buckled round your waist, with the breastplate of righteousness in place, and with your feet fitted with the readiness that comes from the gospel of peace."* Paul uses the word "stand," meaning be ready for action, four times in four verses and adds, *"Be alert"* (v 18). When Peter called to Jesus across the stormy sea *"Tell me to come to you,"* without hesitating Jesus said *"Come!"* (Matthew 14:28-29). The starting point was Peter's suggestion. That sums it up. Jesus says "come" when we want to come and tell him we are ready. Jesus did not ask Peter to walk on the sea until Peter showed that he wanted to do so.

Bible men of God never prayed about going; they just went. God does not make us willing, never tampers with our will. His will for us is not rigid. He has no strict pattern which we must earnestly seek and to which we must strive to conform. Christianity is not that hard. Some Christians live in a state of anxiety or uncertainty, wanting to obey, always seeking, but never sure that they have understood God's plan for them or if they have somehow missed the way. The Bible teaches no such thing. God harmonizes with our will, like two people walking along the road agreeing with one another as they go. When Jesus walked with the two disciples on the Emmaus road after his resurrection, it was at their suggestion that he went home with them.

God does not do what he calls us to do, nor does God do what we call him to do. It is a joint affair of fellow-laborers. We can take the gospel to the people and he leaves that to us. Much praying will never get God to do what we should do. Some describe revival as God entering the field and taking over, while we watch. The New Testament suggests nothing of the kind. The gospel is not news when nobody tells it. God does not proclaim the good news about himself all by himself. We are the proclaimers.

Beginning is half the task and often the hardest part of the task. There are sleeping individuals and sleeping churches. In Revelation Jesus warns the churches in Asia that are resting on their oars and letting the current take them.

The Book of Proverbs was written *"for attaining wisdom and acquiring a disciplined and prudent life"* (Proverbs 1:2-3). 6 times this powerful book warns the "sluggard" and 11 times the slothful and sleepers. A repeated maxim is *"How long will you lie there, you sluggard? When will you get up from your sleep? A little sleep, a little slumber, a little folding of the hands to rest – and poverty will come on you like a bandit"* (Proverbs 6:9-11). We can be very active looking after ourselves but in kingdom interests we can be non-starters.

"Whatever he tells you, do it!" That is all God wants and he gives the boost and the effectiveness. Paul wanted to rouse a sleeping church and said, *"The hour has come for you to wake up from your slumber because salvation is nearer now than when we first believed"* (Romans 13:11) – referring to the coming of Christ, which is 2,000 years nearer now. To the church at Ephesus he quoted, *"Wake up, O sleeper, rise from the dead, and Christ will shine on you"* (5:14) and then commented, *"Be very careful, then, how you live, making the most of every opportunity"* (v 15).

God can save souls through us wherever we go and on whatever business. He tells us to do all things in his name – just live, in his name. Living a Christ-like life, without jumping onto a platform, is a major channel, a carrier-wave of the Holy Spirit and truth.

Do not wait to be given a special task. All work for Jesus is special. Some wait, quite sure the Lord has a special task lined up for them, superior to folk engaged in the basic tasks of Christian service. "Menial" is not a word found in the kingdom dictionary. Giving somebody a cup of cold water ranks high in the honors list.

A thousand Forms

Evangelism has a thousand forms. It is not one specified task or means. Paul not only worked with his hands; when the shipwrecked crew got ashore, he went gathering wood for a fire to warm them all. The Holy Spirit can use any activity. The kingdom of God would be very quiet if there were only evangelists and preachers. An army of people is needed alongside those who have the core job of proclaiming the gospel.

When you find the Lord you find occupation. Every hand is needed in the harvest – as is every skill. When Jesus wanted men to fish men, he chose fishermen. When he wanted somebody to teach, he chose Paul, a teacher. When he wanted a spokesman, he chose Peter, who would always jump in and say something. Whatever we do, it is the basis for his call. He made us specially for it.

Some people love to tell us what the Lord is saying to the church today. Do they need to tell us? Can't the church hear? If God has something important to say, he will say it so we do hear it. It is surely not a secret. It seems arrogant for some to suggest that they have the secret vouchsafed to them only, as if they were more intimate with the Lord, rare spiritual individuals.

Jesus' last instructions to us were *"Go into all the world and preach the good news"* (Mark 16:15). That was to be the substantial function of the Church on earth. Has he had a better idea since then? He gave us no hint that he would later have some secret new instructions channeled outside the word through special individuals.

> The gospel is not news when nobody tells it. God does not proclaim the good news about himself all by himself. We are the proclaimers.

There are no instant courses in evangelism. There is a regular stream of suggestions, ideas, innovations, means, and methods for instant revival or swift success. If we forget the "instant," they can be tools for us to use. One thing is sure, however: they do not produce results without us. Churches may be geared to a particular church growth scheme but unless we are careful, winning men and women for Christ becomes subsidiary, no longer direct. Everything is put into the scheme, everyone recruited to work the machine. God uses many means and many different people, and it is sad to see good workers distracted from the work they are best able to do. New methods adapted to the times or to circumstances are tools of service; the danger is that they become the service itself.

God blesses all who join him in his own major work of salvation. He created each of us with an individual personality for his own purposes. It is noticeable that he blessed the go-ahead man or woman, the resourceful, the enterprising, the people of zest. He looks for people to give themselves as they are and he will make them what he wants them to be, whether they are super-intelligent or simple.

Jesus said, *"Follow me!"* When we tell people to follow Jesus, we usually mean spiritually. For his disciples it meant real walking. Jesus led them here, there and everywhere to meet the unwanted and unwashed, to befriend the poor and the rich, and to care about the riff-raff or rulers.

To follow Jesus spiritually will sooner or later mean actually. Jesus did not obey the Father in a "religious" way only. It meant putting his feet on the road. We will go where he would like to go, meet those he would like meet. The sinless man identified with sinners and bore their reproach. He calls us to leave the Christian ghetto and to share the concerns of real people. That is how believers become real themselves, not cardboard cut-out Christians. If we truly follow him, we become like him. If we know him well, stick close to him, his accent and his ways will brush off on us and, without even knowing it. Anybody can be the real thing, including you.

Questions

1. What would you like to do for God? Why aren't you doing it? Are you doing something while you are waiting?
2. God harmonizes his will with your will. Is your will something with which God can harmonize?

Part 3

Anyone who has faith in me
will do what I have been doing.
He will do even greater things than these,
because I am going to the Father.
He will give you another Counselor
– the Spirit of truth.

John 14:12,16

CHAPTER 11

What "Greater Things"?

"You will do even greater things than these."
John 14:12

How could anyone do greater things than Christ?

The more deeply we delve into Christ's deeds and words, the more they open up with fresh truth. The word itself is a fruitful garden of ever-fresh beauty. Jesus was never commonplace, saying the obvious: *"The words of the Lord are flawless, like silver refined in a furnace of clay, purified seven times"* (Psalm 12:6).

What Jesus says in John 14:12 is extraordinary: *"I tell you the truth, anyone who has faith in me will do what I have been doing. He will do even greater things than these, because I am going to the Father."* It challenges our conceptions and we wonder if we can attain it.

Christ's healing wonders have continued in the ministry of his people though nobody has seen "greater things," but his natural miracles have never been repeated. Some 150 gallons of well-water turned into sparkling wine, 5,000 fed with a boy's packed lunch, walking on the sea through a storm: they remain hallmarks of the Son of God. Jesus healed the blind, deaf and crippled and those acts still represent his physical work.

So what did he mean by "greater things"?

First, let us look at the context. The words occur as part of his discourse on the Comforter, the Holy Spirit. He told us that without the Holy Spirit we can achieve nothing but that by the Spirit we can do whatever he tells us, including healing diseases and expelling demons. Then he promises us the same Spirit as he had received from the Father: *"Unless I go away, the Counselor will not come to you; but if I go, I will send him to you. I have much more to say to you, more than you can now bear. But when he, the Spirit of truth, comes, he will guide you into all truth"* (John 16:7,12-13).

The Dynamics of Pentecost

That is the background to the amazing statement *"Anyone who has faith in me will do what I have been doing. He will do even greater things than these, because I am going to the Father. He will give you another Counselor – the Spirit of truth"* (John 14:12,16). No juggling with that verse can render it less startling. If we look at the Greek for a clue, we find that the word just means "greater." Jesus meant what we understand him to say.

It is his mention of "another Counselor" that sheds some light on the matter. Jesus did not promise "a counselor" but "the Counselor ... another Counselor," who would be with us as he was with his disciples, empowering, guiding, and teaching. With Christ by their side the disciples cast out demons and healed the sick and with the Holy Spirit by their side they would continue the same ministry. That happened, which is, of course, what the Book of Acts is about, but that was only the beginning. The second Book of Acts is still being written.

Jesus was anointed by the Holy Spirit and became the role model for all who receive the Spirit (see Luke 4:18). *"God anointed Jesus of Nazareth with the Holy Spirit and power and he went around doing good and healing all who were under the power of the devil"* (Acts 10:38). With him, things took place that had never been seen before on this earth. Nobody had cast out demons or restored the blind, deaf and crippled to full health. Jesus said that these wonders were the works of the Father and that his followers would do them too.

The Holy Spirit, the promise of Jesus and the promise of the Father, broke into the world and 120 disciples were all Spirit-filled on the day of Pentecost, the dynamic of the Christian faith proving that *"the kingdom of God is not a matter of talk but of power"* (1 Corinthians 4:20).

The first sign of the disciples doing what Jesus did comes in Acts 3:1-10, where we are told of a man who had been born crippled being given the power to walk. He entered the temple, which had once been forbidden for him, *"walking and jumping and praising God"*. Since that time God has not stopped being the Deliverer, setting the multitudes free. Psalm 136:4 says that he *"alone does great wonders."* The world is full of stories. Even my own Gospel Crusades in Africa read like a supplement to the Acts of the Apostles.

However, the healing hand of Jesus is not all he promised. There were to be *"greater things."* Since Jesus made this promise, we would expect to see it fulfilled, so we might ask where and when? What has anyone done that Jesus did not do? The question also arises about what he said in Mark 9:1: *"I tell you the truth, some who are standing here will not taste death before they see the kingdom of God come with power."* The original Greek is *"having come in power."* They would see kingdom power at work. Did they see it before they died?

They did indeed! Paul spoke that way: *"The kingdom of God is not a matter of talk but of power"* (1 Corinthians 4:20). He also prayed for the Ephesians to see *"his incomparably great power for us who believe. That power is like the working of his mighty strength, which he exerted in Christ when he raised him from the dead"* (Ephesians 1:19-20). They saw kingdom power from the day of Pentecost onwards.

Multitudes turning to God

So what were the "greater things"? One thing they did (and which we do) which Jesus never did was to preach the gospel and see a multitude turn to God. This is far greater in every sense than to walk on water or to feed 5,000 with a small boy's lunch. Peter received the promised power from on high, immediately preached the gospel and 3,000 repented and turned to God.

Neither Jesus nor any other preacher had been rewarded with such a result. Noah preached warnings but only his family was saved. Eloquent Isaiah, with his offers and entreaties, achieved nothing. Jeremiah pleaded tearfully, but in vain. Moses led rebellious Israelis to freedom but never saw repentance among the troublesome tribes. Multitudes listened open-mouthed to Christ's every word and ate his miracle bread, but no one cried out for salvation. That moment had not come, for the Spirit had not yet come.

The order changed when Christ sent the Holy Spirit. The disciples had seen Christ's empty tomb and some testified that Jesus was alive, but at first most of them refused to believe. When the Holy Spirit came upon them, all doubts were banished. It was that Spirit-anointing which convinced them and sent them out boldly declaring Jesus was alive. Before he was crucified Jesus had promised that he would send the Spirit and he kept his promise. The Holy Spirit was an unimaginable experience, beyond imitation or self-inducement. It transformed the disciples. Like Moses' burning bush, the fire of God flamed in their soul in the spiritual wilderness of the first century.

Peter had feared the people but now the people feared the Lord, crying out to be saved. This is important. Today, this Christian age has become the day of salvation, by the presence of God's Spirit. Without that work of the Spirit, prophets had exhorted sinners in vain to repent. With the Spirit *"a little child will lead them"* (Isaiah 11:6).

Every Christian today is plunged into a special situation. We are in the latter days and God has chosen us and equipped us by his Spirit. He depends on us. Believers are his only means. We are his resurrection witnesses, human pieces of evidence of the powers of an age to come.

Jesus depends on us. Believers are **his** only means. We are his resurrection witnesses, human pieces of evidence of the powers of **his** coming age.

Today, "ministries of deliverance" abound, offering miracle release from every real or imaginary bondage, spiritual, psychological, demonic, acquired, or inherited. However, *"greater things"* in John 14 is about the saving of souls. That was the work that Jesus called *"greater."* It is wonderful to expel alien spirits in Christ's name, but Jesus said, *"Do not rejoice that the spirits submit to you, but rejoice that your names are written in heaven"* (Luke 10:20). He himself gave them the power of exorcism, but new names written in heaven were supreme.

> Jesus depends on us. Believers are his only means. We are his resurrection witnesses, human pieces of evidence of the powers of his coming age.

Our gospel is not an opportunity for the spectacular but to convey the love of God to a sinful world by the indwelling power and love of the heavenly Counselor.

Questions

1. Why didn't Elijah or any of the prophets of the Biblical canon see converts or healings like the disciples?
2. The word is the gospel. What would render it powerless?

The Lord did not set his affection
on you and choose you because you were
more numerous than other peoples,
for you were the fewest of all peoples.
But it was because the Lord loved you.

Deuteronomy 7:7

CHAPTER 12

God's good Character

"I live by faith in the Son of God,
who loved me and gave himself for me."

Galatians 2:20

What is God like?

The most important Bible question of all is "What is God like?" Getting the answer right will clear up many questions and correct false teaching. The words of Paul came into my mind: *"the Son of God, who loved me."* That apostle, a towering intellectual, truly knew God and his Son our Lord Jesus. His reaction is moving: *"The Son of God loved me and gave himself for me."* He just loved Jesus. His words are full of feeling as well as of teaching. The whole Bible is like that, simple yet profound, full of truths that anyone can understand and with other truths springing from them.

Ideas about God have always abounded – he is a big subject! Today everyone seems to have their own ideas about him. Who is right? The answer is simple. To know what is right, we go back to the book that first told us about him, the Bible. God cannot be different from what the Bible says or he would not be God.

There are alternative ideas which are based on isolated Bible texts; they follow human reasoning and even Greek pagan thinkers who were around before Christ. These were the "classical" theories, traditional beliefs that deeply affected the church, its dogmas, the lives of generations, and even the course of nations. They did not inspire evangelism. We have no room to contend with philosophic ideas about God – and nor do we wish to. Everything in this chapter and this book rests foursquare on Scripture as the revealed word of God. It does not pirouette on a few isolate texts quoted as "evidence." The Bible-wide picture in this chapter and the rest of this book has always provided the impulse to reach people for God. Our own Christ for All Nations campaigns have won tens of millions for Jesus already. Jesus said that the Scriptures all spoke of him and that he is what the Father is.

So, we began with Paul's moving words about the Son of God who *"loved me and gave himself for me."* That is what God is like. He is not an abstract power or a far-off being sitting in splendid indifference, beyond feelings and beyond the reach of anything that would affect him. He is a loving, active, responsive Lord Jesus. From the opening chapters of Scripture God is shown to be personal, concerned and approachable. When Adam sinned, God went looking for him. He had lost him and missed him. He wanted to find him like a man looks for a friend or a son.

The Bible love poem, The Song of Solomon, conveys the amazing significance of God seeking love. Jesus also said that God seeks those who worship (love) him. That is what God is like – he interacts with us, acknowledges us mortals. He is not a king riding past in glory and splendor but a friend knocking at our door asking, "May I come in?" He sustains personal relationships with us. We have fellowship with him and he with us. In surprising ways he depends on us, and all our dependence is on him. He saves us and trusts us to serve him. His love is better than wine and he wants his love requited. We rejoice in him, and he rejoices in us even when we approach him as sinful creatures repenting. It sets all heaven dancing.

The doors of his royal audience chamber stand open to us day and night. The Bible tells us all that time and again. We talk to him and he walks with us. We pray; he hears. Prayer moves the hand that moves the world. The ancients who wrote the Psalms cried to God to awake, rouse himself, and come down to make a difference in their world. That is how they understood him – openhearted and open-handed.

In the Dark Ages it was taught that human distress could not affect God for if it did he would not be perfect. That teaching is still around today. It is dreadful logic, a fallacy. The Bible tells us all the time that our troubles and joys reach God. The whole purpose and truth of the gospel declares it. God so loved us! Love without feeling is not the love of God and is not love at all.

"We do not have a high priest who is unable to sympathize with our weaknesses, but we have one who has been tempted in every way" (Hebrew 4:15). The Greek word for "sympathize" is *sumpatheo* but the word is more than sympathize. It is more like empathize – "to suffer with," "to engage in suffering." That is the awful reality of the cross. Jesus bore our sins, was our scapegoat, made sin for us; he knew what it was like to be a sinner. Yet God was in Christ in those hours.

> God cannot be different from what the Bible says or he would not be God.

A young wife left her home and went out to become a sex slave. A dozen reactions, unspeakable distress, tore the soul of her husband apart. He was Hosea the prophet. God then moved in on Hosea's grief and emphasized that he felt the same way about unfaithful Israel: *"How can I give you up, Ephraim? My heart is changed within me; all my compassion is aroused. I will not carry out my fierce anger for I am God, and not man – the Holy One among you"* (Hosea 11:8-9). God changed his plans because he was not a man.

Jeremiah was called the weeping prophet, his tears a prophetic reflection of God's tears. Ephraim was his grief, too: *"Is not Ephraim my dear son, the child in whom I delight? My heart yearns for him; I have great compassion for him"* (Jeremiah 31:20). If this is not real but only a way of speaking, then it is horribly deceptive. God exposes his essence to us in such verses.

God is not impassive like a corpse unsusceptible to hurt. He is a living God. Between him and his creatures is a live nerve, an umbilical cord. He is not shut into himself and his own thoughts for *"in him we live and move and have our being. We are his offspring,"* said Paul quoting from the Greek poets Cleanthus and Aratus. God holds us close to his heart and senses our very thoughts.

This is our God

He is beside us when we work and witness. When we pray he says, "Amen!" In fact, he is the Amen (Revelation 3:14). Our prayers are not answered by our producing an effect on ourselves, a kind of rebound. If we pray, he hears us and things happen. If we do not pray, nothing happens. Some say that answers to prayer are only coincidences, but those who do not pray have no coincidences. Prayer moves God. If that is not true, then the Bible misleads us.

Moses interceded for Israel when God said that he would destroy them and start a new race with Moses. He yielded to Moses' pleas and was turned away from what he had first planned to do (Deuteronomy 9). Abraham also pleaded with the Lord for the cities of the plain, and God said that he would do what Abraham asked (Genesis 18:16-33). That is clear teaching on the subject of prayer from the foundation of all we believe. God had come down disturbed by the wickedness of Sodom and the cities of the plain, just as he had been angered by the corruptions in the antediluvian world, even saying that he regretted making people.

Our Lord Jesus came to reveal God to us – and wept; people saw that he was moved with compassion. Jesus said that he had often wanted to protect Jerusalem's people but they would not let him. They stopped him from giving them what he longed to give and he wept broken-heartedly.

Christ saves those who believe and we preach to bring them to faith, no matter how men reason about God. God *"is patient, not wanting anyone to perish, but everyone to come to repentance"* (2 Peter 3:9).

God himself never changes. God is eternally the same in nature, character and disposition. What he says he is, he always is. *"He remains faithful for ever"* (Psalm 146:6). God encourages us to pray and to believe that he is always there, unchangeably waiting to help and bless us, open to us every day. He is always willing and never unwilling.

When human affairs anger the Lord, we can ask him to show mercy as Moses did, believing that the heart of God was always seeking reconciliation. We affect God. We can grieve him, quench the Spirit, provoke him, anger him and even deny him but we can never change what he is.

We change our minds about many things because we are changeable beings. There are ways in which God never changes. Anyone who really loves and accepts love is not a stone mountain, unmovable and unfeeling. God is a true Father and responds to us in love. *"We love because he first loved us"* (1 John 4:19). Our love is a reflection of his love, like the mighty sun reflected in a pocket mirror. Evangelism is one of the ways in which we express God's love. No wife says, "I have made a commitment to talk about my husband." She just does it. Jeremiah said, *"If I say, 'I will not mention him or speak any more in his name', his word is in my heart like a fire, a fire shut up in my bones"* (Jeremiah 20:9). To him, prophecy was not a well-deliberated decision but a burning necessity.

> He is beside us when we work and witness. When we pray he says, "Amen!" In fact, he is the Amen.

That is the Lord God, the Jesus we preach. Our gospel is not made up of cryptic teachings issued by some guru in a cave. It is Jesus! Who else has arms extended to the unloved of the nations?

How God makes himself known

Now I want to talk about the Lord as I see him in both the Old and New Testaments. He said that all the Scriptures spoke of him. We see his eyes behind the lattice lines of print. Nobody says that Jesus was like God. God is like him. He is our highest thought of God. *"I am in the Father and the Father is in me. The words I say to you are not just my own. Rather, it is the Father, living in me, who is doing his work"* (John 14:10). His origins are clear: *"I came from the Father and entered the world"* (John 16:28). One disciple described him as *"the radiance of God's glory and the exact representation of his being"* (Hebrew 1:3). The apostle Paul, once full of hate for Jesus, met him and declared, *"We have the light of the knowledge of the glory of God in the face of Christ"* (2 Corinthians 4:6).

God made himself known through Moses in a way never revealed to Abraham. God makes himself known through Jesus in a way not revealed to Moses. Jesus said, *"I and the Father are one. Anyone who has seen me has seen the Father"* (John 10:30, 14:9). The world will be what it believes about God. The knowledge of him transmitted through Moses killed superstition and was the hope of a world of freedom. The knowledge of Christ spells a world free of blind hatred, a world of peace, happiness and decency. He is the Prince of Peace. To present him, we project the hope of a good world.

When I preach, I often think that there could be potential tyrants listening, even as children: Hitlers, Stalins, Chairman Maos, Bin Ladens, and their evil henchmen. The gospel can save them and save the world. The Bible God is love. If the world believed in a God like that, a God like Jesus Christ, what a wonderful world it would be!

After Moses saw the burning bush, he went to Sinai and received the Ten Commandments, not one of them with a threat attached. Jesus quoted the first commandment and Deuteronomy 6:5:

"Love the Lord your God with all your heart and all your soul and all your strength." This is a most startling thought – he is a God who wants to be loved!

God revealed first his nature to Moses. He said, *"I have indeed seen the misery of my people in Egypt. I have heard them crying out because of their slave drivers, and I am concerned about their suffering. So I have come down to rescue them"* (Exodus 3:7-8). Why would he want to do that? He talked about *"my people."* My people! Worshippers of the gods of Egypt! It was inexplicable; except that he was so big that he embraced them all.

The words in Deuteronomy 7:7 are heart-warming: *"The Lord did not set his affection on you and choose you because you were more numerous than other peoples, for you were the fewest of all peoples. But it was because the Lord loved you."* He loved them. Why? Because he did.

That is God. Israel later proved to be rebellious and intractable and troubled him greatly. Yet when they were in their most provocative mood, he said, *"I have loved you with an everlasting love, I have drawn you with loving kindness"* (Jeremiah 31:3). When God wants to convey any truth to us, he usually does it by deeds, actions, but in that verse it is a declaration of passion. It seems as if he could not help but say it.

Nonetheless, he acted, too. He unleashed the powers of creation against Egypt. Moses spoke of it as *"the favor of him who dwelt in the burning bush"* (Deuteronomy 33:16). Frightening as it was, it proved God's favor to a world of ignorance and oppression.

Real love is selfless and does not look for profit. He pours out love on all people like the sun pours out light on the evil and the just. The sun feels nothing but God's love is an infinite depth of feeling. Evangelism demonstrates it whether people are well disposed or not. Nothing puts him off, not even death by crucifixion. *"Having loved his own, he loved them to the last"* (John 13:1).

Gods' character cannot change. In the book of deliverance, Exodus, he used the two words *"I will"* 92 times. The original meaning of those words implied a decision but in Scripture they suggest a desire, "I want to." In Isaiah chapters 40-46 God uses the same words 46 times. In those chapters another expression is joined – *"I"* – and God uses it 126 times insisting on his steadfast character. Sometimes he says *"I, even I."* He declares that he is faithful. To Moses he said, *"I am who I am"* (Exodus 3:14) and in Isaiah he makes the point even clearer: *"I am the Lord, and there is no other"* (Isaiah 45:6).

We can proclaim him everywhere, for ever. He is what he said about himself. He does not change. He is faithful to himself, to his own self-revelation. And so is Jesus. The Jesus of yesterday, of Galilee and Jerusalem, loving, healing, dying for us and raised from the dead, also says, "I, even I." There is only one Jesus, the Jesus of the Gospels, saving, healing, dying and raised to immortal life. If we preach a Jesus who no longer performs works of compassion, we are preaching another Jesus – and why should we want to do that? The Jesus we talk about is *"the same yesterday and today and forever"* (Hebrew 13:8). Preach the Bible Jesus!

"Yes" and "Amen"

Paul told the Corinthians that the Old Testament promises are "Yes" and "Amen" in Christ Jesus (1 Corinthians 1:20). They were covenant promises to Israel but have been ratified by Christ for us all. Paul told the Ephesian elders that he had proclaimed the *"whole will of God"* (Acts 20:27), that is the whole word of God. His word is God's *"I will"* for ever settled in heaven.

"I will" ties bride and bridegroom together. God's *"I will"* embraces us all. To Israel he declared, *"Your Maker is your husband"* (Isaiah 54:5). When God says "I will" nothing can deflect him from his purpose. He said, *"I will pour out my Spirit on all people"* (Joel 2:28) and he is doing that, despite unbelief and opposition.

He said, *"Whoever comes to me I will never drive away"* (John 6:37) and he never does. He stakes his reputation, his name, on his character. When he made a convent with Abraham, *"since there was no one greater for him to swear by, he swore by himself"* (Hebrew 6:13). We are safe!

His disposition matches his nature and character. Disposition is a person's personality. What is he like to be with? The Psalmist said, *"You will fill me with joy in your presence, with eternal pleasures at your right hand"* (Psalm 16:11). God's temperament is joy and exuberant happiness. He is an eternal fountain bubbling up with the spirit of gladness.

Jesus spoke the language of the field workers, of wives, and of laborers, which is why they listened. He spoke of profound things yet in language so full of imagery that people had to smile.

The God who made our world brimmed over with joy as he did it. The trees of the field dance in the winds. He put the antics into animals playing, even in elephants, giraffes, ducks, kittens, squirrels and monkeys! His world is full of color, pleasure, excitement and surprise. I noticed that the Bible simply mentions that *"he also made the stars"* (Genesis 1:16) – as if by a casual gesture.

My God is a sea of hilarious surprises. Sarah said, *"God has made me laugh"* (Genesis 21:6) and he has been making people laugh ever since. However, God has often been misrepresented. So often, worshippers switch off their smiles when they enter a church, although Jesus said, *"Come and share your master's happiness"* (Matthew 25:21,23).

What makes God happy? Well, he is always happy, but Jesus said, *"There is rejoicing in the presence of the angels of God over one sinner who repents"* (Luke 15:10). It does not say that the angels have joy although no doubt they do; the joy is *"in their presence."* God's angels see his joy.

When we are what Jesus meant us to be, fishers of men, God will say, *"Well done, good and faithful servant. Come and share your master's happiness."* Share his world concern and share his joy. There are countless pleasures and joys in every life, despite everything the devil can throw at us. God is always the winner and so are we when his presence is with us and we know him.

Questions

1. If God responds to us, which means a change in him, in what way is he unchanging?
2. Can you think of ways in which we affect God?

CHAPTER 13

What do we need to know?

"They will all know me!"
Jeremiah 31:34

Without God our lives are without meaning. To know him is everything.

Without God we are linked to nothing, like scraps of paper blowing in the wind. God made us for himself, not for ourselves. He did not drop us off in this world like Robinson Crusoe castaways, abandoned and forgotten, leaving us to get on with it the best we can. He retains ownership of us and has a purpose for each of us.

"Man's chief end is to glorify God, and to enjoy him for ever," says the Westminster Catechism. While enjoyment is part of the package, God is not there just for our selfish enjoyment, our convenience. We are there for him. *"All things were created by him and for him"* (Colossians 1:16). It is a two-way process, a partnership which is expected to give us joy.

The God of Love and Joy

Nobody knows what it is like to know God until they do. Yet we have nothing to fear; the Psalmist assures us that we are not in for an unpleasant surprise: *"Taste and see that the Lord is good"* (Psalm 34:8).

Knowing God is the beginning of the journey and the end. We begin in him and end in him. The first verse of Mark's Gospel declares that Jesus Christ **is** the good news – Jesus, not just what he did, his "usefulness," but he himself, *"Immanuel,"* which means *"God with us"* (Matthew 1:23). What more could we ask?

> Without God
> we are linked to nothing,
> like scraps of paper
> blowing in the wind.
> God made us
> for himself,
> not for ourselves.

His advent was everything, and nothing makes sense without him. He was the event to crown all events.

Jesus came down to earth – he breached the barrier between human beings and God and reached out to the untouchables. His coming raised the share value of human beings to infinity. We are the most valuable creatures that God ever made because we cost God his Son, who willingly sacrificed himself for us. God lavished *"his great love"* on us (Ephesians 2:4). That "great love" was not an emotion but a person, his Son; God loved us through and with him. What else could we ask for, what higher tribute can we pay ourselves than to take Jesus into our lives? *"What is man that you are mindful of him, the son of man that you care for him?"* (Psalm 8:4).

However, what is so impressive is not merely that he came down to our humble life form but what he did when he came. It added gold upon gold, layer upon layer. *"We are in him who is true – even in his Son Jesus Christ. He is the true God and eternal life"* (1 John 5:20). The Bible calls this *"reconciliation"* (2 Corinthians 5:19). It is not about anything we did, but the result of an initiative taken by God himself: *"God reconciled us to himself"* (2 Corinthians 5:18). The amazing thing is that he did this when we were hostile to him, *"while we were still sinners"* (Romans 5:8). Jesus did not come to save the godly but the ungodly. The depths of God are unfathomed; his amazing dimensions are evident from the fact that he stepped down from glory to join us and accepted all that it involved.

Let me take you through Scripture to show you what the Old Testament godly said even before Christ came to earth: *"You will fill me with joy in your presence, with eternal pleasures at your right hand"* (Psalm 16:11); *"You have filled my heart with greater joy than when their corn and new wine abound"* (Psalm 4:7);

"Love the Lord your God with all your heart and with all your soul and with all your strength" (Deuteronomy 6:5); *"As the deer pants for streams of water ,so my soul pants for you, O God"* (Psalm 42:1); *"My heart and flesh cry out for the living God"* (Psalm 84:2). Moses prayed, *"Now show me your glory"* (Exodus 33:18) and God told Abraham, *"I am your very great reward"* (Genesis 15:1).

God allowed Moses to see him but not to see his face (Exodus 33:23). In the New Testament John the apostle said, *"The Word became flesh. We have seen his glory"* (John 1:14). The great promise for the dying is that *"they will see his face"* (Revelation 22:4); for the living the promise is that the pure in heart *"will see God"* (Matthew 5:8). The apostles saw Jesus but Peter wrote to those who had not had that privilege that they were *"filled with an inexpressible and glorious joy"* (1 Peter 1:8). Paul wrote, *"To me, to live is Christ"* (Philippians 1:21). He considered *"everything a loss compared to the surpassing greatness of knowing Christ Jesus, his Lord"* (Philippians 3:8). We need to appreciate that when John wrote *"We have seen his glory, the glory of the One and Only, who came from the Father, full of grace and truth,"* it immediately showed who he was talking about, for grace and truth are the two great statements about God shown to Moses in Exodus 34:6-7.

We should not move so much as an inch from this truth. It is the pivot around which we orbit. Christ is the beginning and the end. He is the way and the destination, the road as well as where it goes. Our teaching is true, that we are sinners and that Christ died for our sins to save us. However, that is information and believing it is a mental act. Yet it is *"with your heart that you believe and are justified"* (Romans 10:10). Faith is an act, an attitude, a decision. We are not saved by faith in an idea, something we do, but by faith in what he does. Jesus saves! What is more, he saves us so that we can know him.

The gospel begins with forgiveness but that is not the end. The way is cleared so that we can be *"brought near through the blood of*

Christ" (Ephesians 2:13) – near to God, that is. The object of salvation is fellowship with him. We may be proud to know a famous person but to know Christ is more than knowing royalty. Millions have given up everything for Jesus, even their lives. To know him is everything.

"They will all know me!" (Jeremiah 31:34). This is God's word through the prophet Jeremiah. Ezekiel contains some 70 references to knowing the Lord. It is repeated 7 times in Exodus. Personal relationship with God is the most blessed of all experiences, fulfilling our deepest instincts and desire.

> God lavished *"his great love"* on us. That *"great love"* was not an emotion but a person, his Son; God loved us through and with him.

Jeremiah prophesied, *"Let not the wise man boast of his wisdom or the strong man boast of his strength or the rich man boast of his riches, but let him who boasts boast about this: that he understand and knows me, that I am the Lord"* (Jeremiah 10:4). Knowing God is the matchless wonder of Christianity. There are no competitors. No holy book of any other religion contains such words. It is not a promise for some far future but experience for today. To know him, is eternal life: *"Now this is eternal life: that they may know you, the only true God, and Jesus Christ, whom you have sent"* (John 17:3). *"He is the true God and eternal life"* (1 John 5:20).

In the Hebrew Scriptures there is no word for "presence"; "face" is used instead. Hebrew uses concrete, rather than abstract, expressions. Pharaoh told Moses, *"See my face no more"* (Exodus 10:28). Seeing the face of God means knowing that God is present.

The New Testament speaks of being in God's presence. *"God made his light shine in our hearts to give us the light of the knowledge of the glory of God in the face* [presence] *of Christ"* (2 Corinthians 4:6). *"They will see his face"* – be in his presence (Revelation 22:4).

The Object of Evangelism

That is the object of evangelism. It is not a signs and wonders show. However great the mercy of God in physical deliverance, in healing, the primary purpose is for people to know the Lord. We can believe in miracles but not in Jesus. The mighty works which take place in our meetings are not to make people say "Oh!" but to make them say, "Oh Lord, I want to know you. Save me!" *"Though you have not seen him, you love him; and even though you do not see him now, you believe in him and are filled with an inexpressible and glorious joy"* (1 Peter 1:8).

If we follow his teaching, it always leads us back to him. He is what he taught. He did not bring us a road map to follow for a lifetime so as to ending up at "Destination God." He said, *"Come to me. I am the way."* The Bible has no abstract ideas about God. He appears to us in the living flesh of Christ.

For thousands of years there was no Bible, nor were there any churches or preachers and God was known only to a few. Through the centuries even Israel only knew the Lord second hand, through the priesthood. Families made pilgrimages to Jerusalem with offerings but priests were their go-betweens. Even Job prayed, *"If only I knew where to find him!"* (Job 23:3).

Chronicles lists families. One man, Jabez, was *"more honorable than his brothers"* and *"cried out to the God of Israel"* (1 Chronicles 4:9-10). The prophets' frequent complaint was that people did not call on the Lord. *"The Lord looks down from heaven on the sons of men to see if there are any who understand, any who seek God. All have turned aside, they have together become corrupt; there is no one who does good, not even one"* (Psalm 14:3).

That is where we come into the picture. We are not theologians and attorneys at law defending Christ. He is not a defendant; he is God! We testify of him and, in fact, do more than testify;

as Paul said, *"We are Christ's ambassadors."* When we promote Jesus, doctrine and evidence may be challenged but testimony is unassailable. Everyone can trust when they cannot think, even the dying. Just as they can take the hand of a loved one, they can take the hand of Jesus.

Knowing the Lord is not merely about taking on a new set of ideas but it does change ideas. It does so because it opens up a different window on life. Receiving Christ does not make our face luminous like Moses' face; we have *"treasure in jars of clay"* (2 Corinthians 4:7). This looks back to Gideon, who formed a tiny army and armored them only with a torch inside a clay jug. When the signal was given, they smashed the pitchers and waved the torches, deceiving the enemy, who panicked, thinking that a vast army had been recruited. We are mundane creatures of clay but the flame of the light of Christ burns in our hearts. The book of Ecclesiastes talks about *"the pitcher shattered at the spring"* (Ecclesiastes 12:6); then our light will blaze out to outshine the stars. No work of man on earth, however wonderful, can produce such an outcome. It is *"Christ in us, the hope of glory"* (Colossians 1:27).

Saul of Tarsus had listened to Stephen's Holy Spirit empowered preaching. He saw the stones crash on his head and break the golden bowl, the pitcher. However, the glory of Stephen followed him while he rampaged on like a fox among chickens, the murder in his heart creating mayhem. Then the glory of Christ blinded him on the Damascus road. When he regained his sight, he knew that he had seen *"the glory of God in the face of Jesus Christ,"* but he first saw that glory in Stephen: *"All who were sitting in the Sanhedrin* [the council] *looking intently at Stephen and they saw that his face was like the face of an angel"* (Acts 6:15).

For long centuries all nations lived in superstition, serving their idols and worshipping the sun, moon, rivers or stars – until Israel got to know the Lord. Civilizations arose – Rome and Greece with its thinkers – but their ladder of logic was too short to reach God. Reason was the tower of Babel which failed to reach heaven. For 2,000 years ignorance of God continued – even after Abraham found the Lord.

The little land of Israel was in the nut-cracker jaws of the great powers to the north and south. Yet Israel survived for one reason – God had deposited with them the world's most wonderful secret, the knowledge of the Lord. Israel was eventually reduced to a mere scattering across Europe, yet the promise was that *"the earth will be full of the knowledge of the Lord as the waters cover the sea"* (Isaiah 11:9). That is happening now; the knowledge of the Lord is advancing right now like an incoming tide across the shores of continents.

We know the Lord through Israel alone. Nobody trusted the gods and "hope" was despised as the sentimentality of senile women. Today the praises of God never end. In Israel before Christ, one person here and there was intimate with the Lord and was named in Scripture: Noah, Abraham, Joseph, Moses and David. Few of them saw anything miraculous but they trusted God. One of these great souls was the national leader of Israel, Ezra. He led a multitude of 50,000 people who had been released from Babylonian captivity and who were carrying a vast hoard of treasure on a 5-months trek through areas where warlords regularly plundered traveling caravanserai. However, Ezra refused a military escort, saying that God would take care of them – and God did.

> We are not theologians and attorneys at law defending Christ. He is not a defendant; he is God! We testify of him.

Ezra never heard God's voice, never had a vision or a dream; he never saw a miracle or had a supernatural experience. His faith in God was based entirely on what he read about him in the Scriptures. The drama ended with the people and treasure safe in Jerusalem, giving us an historic example of divine protection.

> A nation is what individuals make it. For a nation to be reborn, its people must be born again.

Before Ezra, Jeremiah prophesied, *"This is the covenant that I will make with the house of Israel. I will put my law in their minds and write it on their hearts. I will be their God and they will be my people. No longer will a man teach his neighbor, or a man his brother,* saying, 'Know the Lord', because they will all know me from the least of them to the greatest"* (Jeremiah 31:33–34).

In the Old Testament we hear little about individual wickedness. Sin is usually national. The sons carried the sins of their fathers, and they stood or fell together as a family, as tribe or the whole race. The sin of Achan brought the stigma of guilt on his own family and the whole tribe of Judah for generations, eventually leading to other tribes breaking away from Judah. They set up their own religious standards away from Jerusalem and Judah substituted gods for God. This led to their final disaster, removing them from the pages of history and causing them to disappear in the melting pot of time.

God chose Israel as his covenant people and individuals sheltered behind the covenant to do as they liked, as if it gave them carte blanche for wickedness. They kept up the religious ceremonial of the priesthood and the temple but God's prophet said, *"These people honor me with their lips but their hearts are far from me"* (Isaiah 29:13).

Then God spoke through Ezekiel. He declared that God would deal with individuals and not merely the whole covenant people. God would not punish sons for their fathers' sins but *"the soul who sins is the one who will die"* (Ezekiel 18:3).

That changed the situation. Today we have the ultimate situation: *"Here I am! I stand at the door and knock. If anyone hears my voice and opens the door, I will come in and eat with him, and he with me"* (Revelation 3:20). The prophet Joel also pinpointed individuals. He prophesied, *"I will pour out my Spirit on all people. Your sons and daughters will prophesy, your old men will dream dreams, your young men will see visions. Even on my servants, both men and women, will I pour out of my Spirit in those days"* (Joel 2:28-29).

Nicodemus saw Jesus as the One who could deliver Israel. But the nation needed a Savior from sin, not a military lord. John the Baptist was preaching *"The kingdom of God is near"* (Matthew 3:2). John knew that sin was a personal issue and he baptized hundreds in the Jordan for repentance and cleansing from sin. Yet river water could not do it. God gave him a new message that someone was coming who would baptize with fire and the Holy Spirit, not in cold water. Jesus told Nicodemus, *"You must be born of water and the Spirit"* (John 3:5).

A nation is what individuals make it. For a nation to be reborn, its people must be born again. Ordinary people forsake worship and the nation pays the price. This book is being written when the British Government is introducing drastic measures to counter crime, crime now being 50 times worse than in 1950. The Government says that the cause must be tackled. Well, fine. The truth is, however, that they themselves are the cause as much as anybody. Legislation has been based on loose liberal and "politically correct" standards instead of Christian principles, which are absolute –not obsolete.

People all around the world need to know God for themselves; they need a God experience not a church experience. They do not need to watch the fire burning on the altar but know the fire blazing on the altar of their own hearts. Paul speaks of the *"eyes of our heart"* (Ephesians 1:18); we need to "see" with the heart as well as the head. Books convey truth in words, but the truth of God is deeper than words, deeper than poetry. It is life's greatest experience.

Questions

1. What does this chapter tell us about how we can know the Lord?
2. Can you name two people in the Old Testament who knew the Lord personally?
3. Why could God not save sinners by his omnipotent power?

CHAPTER 14

Secrets of the Holy Spirit

"'By my Spirit,' says the Lord."
Zechariah 4:6

This chapter contains all-important revelations about the Holy Spirit which have been hidden under the varnish of church formality for nearly 1,900 years. The Christian faith depends on the Holy Spirit, so we must know who he is and what he does. There is no Christianity without him, no Christ without the Spirit. The Holy Spirit implements the work Jesus did on earth – that is what Christianity is. The Spirit is not a bonus but basic.

The Holy Spirit's work is the most spectacular and prominent of all God's activities, and yet in the past people thought of him as retiring and secret. They imagined him stealing in to soothe us in our moments of distress, a soft breeze to cool our cheek when the going gets hot, or as an incidental helper waiting on the sidelines to be called in if needed.

When John's Gospel began to be circulated, it produced new hunger for the Holy Spirit and for spiritual gifts. About a century after the apostles, a movement emerged called Montanism. Its greatest adherent was Quintus Tertullian, the theologian who included the Holy Spirit in the Godhead and gave us the word "Trinity." Montanists believed God for Holy Spirit manifestations, especially prophecy. The bishops frowned on people prophesying, as they though it would undermine their authority. Eventually, Montanism was condemned by the Church and listed as a heresy.

We only know about the Montanists through the writings of their opponents, but they do appear to have had an understanding of the Holy Spirit. When the Church rejected Montanism, development in teaching on the Holy Spirit was set back. To exclude the claims of the Montanist's prophets, the Church only authorized priests in the apostolic succession to exercise supernatural powers. Furthermore, those powers were limited to the 7 sacraments, which included turning the Communion wafer into the flesh of Christ and bestowing absolution of sins. Otherwise, divine powers were attributed to nobody officially, though some who inflicted extreme hardships, deprivation and physical affliction on themselves were popularly regarded as saints. They were believed to possess healing powers and a healing miracle was evidence to the Church that they could be canonized as saints.

The reaction from this time (circa AD 200) saw worship lose warmth and excitement and become a routine formality. Fervor in worship was shunned as extremism and emotionalism. Physical reactions were despised as "enthusiasm," the word for Greek worshippers possessed by a god. A recent eminent Roman Catholic wrote against "enthusiasm" and included such scenes as Wesley's meetings. It was assumed that the Holy Spirit could come on a man or woman, fill them with his power and make them his temple but that they would experience only a gentle calm, no excitement. This incredible assumption is a prime example of the ignorance of Bible teaching on the Holy Spirit. The effect of the Spirit on the apostles was so visible that onlookers could only suggest that they were drunk.

Natural Evidence of the Super Natural

In distancing itself from Montanism, which claimed the Holy Spirit, the Church shied away from the Spirit as associated with fanatical behavior. The Holy Spirit was not even named in the Creed until the fourth century. Instead of the Spirit, divine power was called "grace." Grace became the operating power in salvation doctrines. Instead of preaching "Jesus saves," people spoke of grace, "Saved by grace alone." The popular hymn *Amazing Grace* does not even mention God. Grace is the heart of traditional theology in large areas of the Church today.[2]

Certain events which came to be called "revivals" were put down to the operation of grace. These "grace" events moving in sovereign mystery were believed to make up the number of the elect. The Welsh revival of 1904 was probably the first revival recognized as being the work of the Holy Spirit rather than grace. It linked up with the beginnings of the Pentecostal move.

The importance of the Spirit was shown in Jesus' saying that blasphemy against Holy Spirit is unforgivable (Luke 12:10). Nonetheless, for centuries the Holy Spirit was thought of as little more than an anonymous religious feeling, akin to awe in a Cathedral, or a mysterious influence affecting us without us knowing it. Harriet Auber's hymn *Our blest Redeemer* speaks of the Spirit resting in humble hearts, imparting sweet influence; his gentle voice is as soft as the evening air, checking every thought and calming every fear. Until the Pentecostals testified to living experiences and the miraculous, the old idea persisted of the Spirit as a pervading atmosphere, the unseen guide and comforter secretly at work.

How do we identify the Spirit? The Father and the Son are recognized by their typical work. The Father bears the hallmark of creation and the Son his life on earth. Both act as God, of course. The hallmark of the Spirit is action in this material world, *"the hand of God"* or *"the finger of God"* performing the will of God, that is the will of Father and Son, and manifesting God's power on earth. He was linked to earth from the beginning, moving across the face of darkness and chaos. He still broods over human chaos and darkness to generate deliverance, healing, answers to prayer, and other divine action among us.

The Holy Spirit is the God of the physical. The Eternal Spirit dwelling in mortal flesh is specifically resurrection life for the body (Romans 8:11). Peter's first gospel sermon said that very thing, declaring Pentecost as the fulfillment of the promise of the Father. Physical signs are natural evidence of the supernatural.

2 Mainly from the works of the great Augustine (born AD 354) who made the word "grace" central rather than the Spirit.

The spiritual-physical character of Christianity was long forgotten. Then 100 years ago, Holy Spirit baptism began touching thousands and then millions of believers as a spiritual and physical experience with utterance in other tongues, a natural evidence of the supernatural. It was exactly what had happened on the first day of Pentecost: *"They were all filled with the Holy Spirit and began to speak in other tongues as the Spirit enabled them"* (Acts 2:4). This opens the door to the whole field of Holy Spirit phenomena. What is impossible if "tongues" are possible?

Spirit baptism sheds new light and gives new depth to all Christian doctrine. Paul's Greek words for the Spirit's gifts are *charismata* and *pneumatika*, "grace things" and "spirit things" (1 Corinthians 12-14). Every gift is by grace, God's favor. The miracle gifts, physical and spiritual, are not winnable, deserved or achievable or they would not be gifts. They are mainly manifestations of healing, verbal gifts and knowledge or subjective gifts.

For centuries the Church claimed the power to make Christians by the sacraments. Scripture shows we become Christians only by the Holy Spirit. Salvation involves the whole Godhead, Father, Son and Spirit. God was in Christ at the cross, and what Christ did the Holy Spirit translates into our salvation experience. Religions are systems, spiritual formula. Christianity is the power of God manifested spiritually and physically. Christ *"dwells in our hearts through faith"* and our bodies are temples of the Holy Spirit (Ephesians 3:17, 1 Corinthians 6:19).

God does not save us by a doctrine or formula. It is the personal work of the Spirit of Christ. Jesus saves – personally, offering himself as a private transaction between a man and God. No ordinance Jesus gave can save us. Baptism does not save but *"to all who received him, to those who believed in his name, he gave the right to become children of God – children born not of natural descent, nor of human decision or a husband's will, but born of God"* (John 1:13).

True Christian witness is by Spirit-filled people. An early Christian father, Irenaeus, called the apostles "Spirit bearers." This should be true of all followers of Jesus. The Spirit alone makes believers and only believers can testify. The Spirit is the only effective element by which we can have an impact on the lives of the godless. There was no impact whatever until the Holy Spirit came on the day of Pentecost. That is what Jesus said: *"Apart from me you can do nothing"* (John 15:5). Our witness is twofold, what we say and what we are. The disciples had to wait for the Holy Spirit before they sailed the seas with the Good News.

On the day of Pentecost the Holy Spirit poured into their lives as a witness to the resurrection of Christ not merely to give them courage but for its personal effects. Peter declared, *"God has raised this Jesus to life, and we all are witnesses of the fact"* (Acts 2:32). Nobody actually saw Christ rise from the dead, but one thing gave the 120 disciples the credentials of true witnesses: they were full of the Holy Spirit. Christ had sent it as he promised, and now everyone heard them prophesying and speaking in tongues.

> For centuries the Church claimed the power to make Christians by the sacraments. Scripture shows we become Christians only by the Holy Spirit.

We do not need to be different from the original witnesses. The first witness was *"a man who was sent from God; his name was John"* – John the Baptist (John 1:6). He witnessed that Christ would baptize in the Holy Spirit and fire. We have no right to witness to any other Christ than the Christ baptizing in the Holy Spirit and fire. He is not a cold water Christ. Our witness goes beyond water baptism. John's baptism was in water but he said that Christ's baptism would be in fire. The word says, *"No one can enter the kingdom of God unless he is born of water and of the Spirit"* (John 3:5).

Jesus had no concept of people witnessing without the Spirit. Even when they were under the stress of persecution, he said, *"you will be given what to say"* – that is, by the Holy Spirit (Matthew 10:19). Evangelistic success does not come about by persuasion, logic or argument but by the Holy Spirit: *"'not by might nor by power, but by my Spirit,' says the Lord Almighty"* (Zechariah 4:6). Of course, our words are needed as they are the vehicles of the work of the Spirit, but true witness proves itself, like the Scriptures. Christ has risen and ascended to heaven and our message and experience must therefore match that.

The Way God is

Father, Son and Spirit work with one another, as if in holy competition to be a servant to the other, subject to one another. Christ worked by the Spirit of God and the Spirit of God is called the Spirit of Christ. The Spirit was sent by the Father and so was Jesus. The Father sent the Spirit because the Son asked for it. It is a Trinity of mutual service, the ideal and divine role model for all our Christian relationships and for all occasions.

When we expel evil spirits or heal the sick, the whole Godhead is behind us, by the will of the Father, through the Holy Spirit, in the name of Jesus. In his authority in the name of Jesus, we experience *"his incomparably great power for us who believe"* (Ephesians 1:19). However, we do not receive independent power or authority. It is always God at work in and through us, and then only according to his will. We are not given a power pack to use as we like. Power comes as it flows from the will of God to us in a permanent flow as we keep open to God as channels. The only man of power for the hour is Jesus Christ. We are only his servants.

The Holy Spirit did not make a world in which he could do nothing. God did not exclude himself from creation; lock himself out of his own house. The Creating Spirit retains his rights as Creator and can order all things as he sees fit in his own world.

He created the earth as a place for prayer and where prayer would be necessary. That is why miracles are possible.

The great example of God at work in the material realm on earth was the deliverance of Israel from Egyptian bondage, which included making a path through the sea. The waters were piled up by *"a strong east wind," "the blast of his nostrils"* (Exodus 14:21, 15:8). The Hebrew for wind, breath or spirit is *ruach*. The equivalent Greek is *pneuma*. Jesus worked his wonders by the Holy Spirit and never otherwise.

> Christ worked by the Spirit of God and the Spirit of God is called the Spirit of Christ. The Spirit was sent by the Father and so was Jesus.

The Spirit never works alone. The Spirit employs physical channels. Only when the Son of God became the Son of Man, incarnate, did the Spirit work freely, through and with Jesus after the Spirit came upon him at his baptism in the Jordan River. Christ testified that the Father did the works, the healings (John 14:10, Acts 10:38).This is an unbreakable law. The Godhead works as one but each Person has a specific role. That is the way God is.

The Spirit is not only power. He is the Spirit of love. God's power is love power. All he does is prompted and arises from his nature of love. Whatever God does expresses his love, for he is love. His ministry is always an outflow of love. Power is his ability but love is his motive. He means our own ministry to be like his, as fountains of the love that God *"has poured out into our hearts by the Holy Spirit"* (Romans 5:5). That love is not our own temperament just raised a few degrees. Our feeble passions can be so mixed with pride, arrogance, or even greed. Alternatively, we can put on Christ so that his nature is revealed in us. It is a deliberate, conscious and constant act.

God is all in all but we ourselves come into the equation. Jesus said we should pray and ask *"whatever you wish"* in connection with his kingdom (John 15:7). God does what we ask. Our will cannot override the divine purpose but he has left his will open and tied it to the will of his believing children: *"His ears are attentive to their cry"* (Psalm 34:15). His ears mean his heart, himself. He is open to us and determines nothing until we make our request. *"My Father will give you whatever you ask in my name. Ask and you will receive"* (John 16:23). That promise would be impossible if God had decided and fixed everything ahead of time.

Emotion is not the Spirit, though his presence creates emotion. God's presence can obviously have many effects. Just as we are affected by the personalities of our friends – sad, humorous, serious or whatever – so we are affected by God in the particular way he may choose to come to us. Even then, the Spirit may be present without any physical impact upon us. His purpose is not sensation. God is not a stimulant or intoxicant to render us happy or to calm us down. He gives us a sound mind but drugs and other stimulants disturb the mind. God is not a drug and does not affect us like a drug or a serum injection. People get high on drugs but not on God.

He imparts the joy of the Lord, which is our strength. It is a natural part of his indwelling. *"Do not get drunk on wine. Instead, be filled with the Spirit"* (Ephesians 5:18). The verse does not say that we ought to be drunk on the Spirit instead of drunk on wine. It is contrast, not comparison. Drunkenness is nothing like the effects of the Holy Spirit. We are his temples, not his inebriates. On the day of Pentecost Peter declared, *"These men are not drunk, as you suppose"* (Acts 2:15). Peter was certainly not drunk. He preached a world-changing message.

The Pentecostal/Charismatic revival has shown us Holy Spirit power more clearly; there is no other power to compare with it. Some speak of grace as an emanation power from God but grace in action is the Holy Spirit, if you like; the Holy Spirit is God's favor being exercised.

Some people have talked of kingdom power as if it was a newly discovered, special and greater power. There is no such thing. Christ said that **all** power was his and that it resides in the Holy Spirit.

The Holy Spirit was the reason for the Ascension of Christ. *"Unless I go away, the Counselor will not come to you"* (John 16:7). The Church has had a weak understanding of both the Spirit and the Ascension. It was almost a blank page in theology. Better understanding dawned with the Pentecostal movement a century ago. Christ ascended physically to give the Holy Spirit physically, the Man Christ Jesus uniting earth and heaven, representing human men and women in heaven, like the ladder set up to heaven in Jacob's dream (John 1:51, Genesis 28:12). The best heaven was released for us all, by the wonderful Spirit of God.

Therefore *"be filled with the Spirit!"*

Questions

1. What was for many years the "missing ingredient" in teaching about salvation?
2. What do we need for effective witness?

I pray that the eyes of your heart
may be enlightened in order that you may know
his incomparably great power for us who believe.
That power is like the working of his mighty strength,
which he exerted in Christ when he raised him from the dead.

Ephesians 1:18-20

CHAPTER 15

When God did nothing

"The Son can do nothing by himself."
John 5:19

Communication

Living beings speak. We were made to communicate with each other. We were made in the image of God. God is the living God and speaks. By contrast, *"the idols of the nations have mouths, but cannot speak"* (Psalm 135:15-16).

God made man in his image and formed our mouth to speak with the intention of forming our relationship with him and with one another. It is an essential aspect of human nature. Animals, on the other side of a gulf, can neither speak nor have personal relationships. *"If we walk in the light, as he is in the light, we have fellowship one with another and the blood of Jesus purifies us from all sin"* (1 John 1:7). This sets out the basis of fellowship, cleansing by the precious blood of the Redeemer. Competition takes the place of fellowship in the secular world.

However, communication is about more than words. We often ask friends, "What do you mean?" We cannot construe from their words what they really want us to know. We understand people better when we know them well. Words rely on the support of gestures and expressions, body language. A smile makes a remark very different. We never read that Jesus smiled, but of course he did and it would naturally have affected how people understood him. He wept at the tomb of Lazarus, and that conveyed something about Jesus that words perhaps could not have done. His tears showed everyone that Jesus loved Lazarus (John 11:35-36).

We can easily misunderstand people unless we know something of their personality and background. Words are a kind of code. We need to know the person who is speaking and what that person is likely to mean.

That is all true of the Bible. We understand it better when we know God, who is behind it. The better we know the Lord, the better we appreciate what he is saying in his word. He speaks to us through the word, and we read and understand it as communication from a friend. How can we know God's intentions in his word if we are indifferent to him? Sometimes in court a person's words are related publicly, but those listening know nothing about the speaker. This court practice is vicious and open to misunderstanding. Handling God's word when we have no relationship with him makes it open to all kinds of misinterpretations.

When we speak, we commit ourselves to someone, and in a sense become responsible for what we say. Others hear us, read us, and take us on trust. God speaks to us; he commits himself to us and waits for our reaction. He "goes public" and accepts the responsibility when we take him on trust.

God speaks with Intentions

The Bible is the word of God. Some open it but do not believe it. They read it without faith, intellectually, critically like literature, like legends, to find out about ancient customs. We can certainly bring our intellect to bear on the Bible and study it, as we might with a letter from a friend. Scripture should be read remembering that God is communicating with us and that his intention is fellowship.

Bible words, like all words, are a kind of code, as I have said. To interpret Bible words we need to have an acquaintance with God, however much we know about the cultural background and history. How we decode the words shows what we are, whether we trust and love the Lord. That is why we need the Holy Spirit to lead us into their truths. He knows the Son perfectly. Jesus said, *"The Spirit will take from what is mine and make it known to you"* (John 16:15). He communicates Jesus in spiritual intimacy, a sense of things too deep for words. The promise is *"You shall know the Lord"* (Hosea 2:20 NKJV).

God's words are also action. God speaks with intentions. He speaks in order to do something for us and to us. When we read the word, our attitude must be open, receptive and submissive. God has a purpose in speaking. Everything in the word is written for us, to equip us, as Paul wrote to Timothy, for every good work (2 Timothy 3:17). His word to us is creative; it puts into us what we cannot obtain anywhere else. It builds us up in the most holy faith and we grow in the grace and knowledge of Christ.

The written word speaks of the Living Word, Christ Jesus. The very person that Bible words had spoken about came to earth. The written code words had meaning and Jesus was the meaning of the Scriptures. He was the explanation, their intention. He showed himself to the disciples *"in all the Scriptures,"* the Living Word communicating the meaning of the written word (Luke 24:27, John 5:39). Christ is the Word, not a coded expression but the express image of the Father. In wonderful love he presented himself as the word. Instead of posting a letter through the letterbox, he comes along and rings the doorbell himself.

> Christ is the Word, not a coded expression but the express image of the Father. In wonderful love he presented himself as the word. Instead of posting a letter through the letterbox, he comes along and rings the doorbell himself.

God's words are "things," acts, not a sound carried away on the wind. They are creative, producing effects, generating a situation. This world is the materialization of the word that he spoke and it is permeated by his creative voice. Jesus said, *"My words will never pass away"* (Luke 21:33). His words are more than thought or information. They are better than words carved in rock, for they exist as life exists, a reality, for ever, ongoing, a state of things which we enter by faith.

Unity of the Word and the Spirit

The word and the Spirit are one. God speaks and the Holy Spirit acts. When God speaks he always tells us something about himself, which is all-important for human life. When God said, *"Let there be light!"* (Genesis 1:3), light came – for ever, not for a moment or day – and we live in that light. His word commands nature and we can live in his word and his word in us.

God's voice is always at work. The DNA molecule controls our physical shape and pattern. It is the voice of the Creator recorded on the DNA spiral nucleus. It determines every creature's life. God's command programmed the order of living things: *"He sustains all things by his powerful word"* (Hebrew 1:3). The Holy Spirit is the creative Spirit, the key player in all divine action.

> When God said, *"Let there be light!"*, light came – for ever, not for a moment or day – and we live in that light.

For 2,000 years the Holy Spirit manifested himself only on rare occasions but waited to play a full part. Then on the day of Pentecost, 50 days after Jesus rose from the dead, it happened. He arrived here to stay, took up residence in his people, his temple. The Spirit is the legacy bequeathed by Christ when he ascended to the Father.

In earlier times, occasional individuals had experiences of the Spirit, but these were brief moments when he came upon them for some particular task. *"The Holy Spirit had not been given, since Jesus had not yet been glorified"* (John 7:39). Today he is fully with us and does not go away.

Actually, only a few miracles are mentioned in the 39 books from Genesis to Malachi. The Gospels and Acts contain the real record of signs and wonders. Before then, Israel made a miraculous escape from Egypt and saw Mount Sinai tremble under the weight of God's presence and the wilderness full of smoke from the fire of God. However, we notice one strange thing. No divine manifestation changed anybody. Pharaoh saw God's wonders but hardened his heart. Israel was led by the pillar of fire but died in the wilderness. Nobody repented. Nobody became thankful. The people hankered only after onions and cucumbers, not after God's presence.

We are now so privileged. We have *"tasted the powers of the coming age"* (Hebrew 6:5). "Tasted!" Moses saw but did he "taste"? He evinced no joy of sins forgiven or life eternal. He watched God's breath divide the Red Sea but never experienced God breathing on him as Jesus breathed on the disciples or as the winds of God blew upon them on the day of Pentecost. It is thought that Moses wrote Psalm 90, but it is not a happy Psalm; the author laments of the shortness of life and fears old age at 70 or 80. Yet the author, Moses, lived to be 120! He saw what we have today but only as a blurred vision.

In earlier times the Spirit of God came and went but Jesus assured the disciples that the Spirit would come to stay. Acts speaks of the disciples continuing their work full of the Spirit. The opening words of the Acts of the Apostles are *"In my former book, Theophilus, I wrote about all that Jesus began to do and teach until the day he was taken up to heaven."* Note that word *"began."* So, up to the day of Jesus' ascension his ministry was only the beginning and would continue.

Now, if he were to continue after he ascended to God, how could it happen? We need not speculate. The last two verses of Mark's Gospel provide the amazing answer. First we read that *"Jesus was taken up into heaven and he sat at the right hand of God"*

(Mark 16:19). Then we are told that the disciples *"went out and preached everywhere, and the Lord worked with them and confirmed his word by the signs that accompanied it"* (Mark 16:20). Risen to God's right hand of power, Christ was at the same time with his disciples wherever they went. Paradoxically also, he called the apostles to be with him but sent them out.

> The gospel is the catalyst for the power of God. Preach the word and it releases the Spirit.

How was this possible? The Holy Spirit was the power in Jesus' ministry. The wonderful truth is that he promised that the same Spirit would rest on those who believed. He would send *"another Counselor"* (John 14:16) to be with those who follow him and to do the works that he did. Jesus' name for the Spirit was "Paraclete" (Greek *allos* + *parakleetos*, "another called alongside to give support"). The Spirit came alongside the disciples as Jesus had done. Christ's work would continue through the disciples, with the same Spirit.

It is wonderful that by the Spirit we can continue the work that Christ began on earth 2,000 years ago. That is what we are here for: *"Whatever you do, whether in word or deed, do it all in the name of the Lord Jesus"* (Colossians 3:17). Acting in his name, we always do his work, not just when we are in church. That means one wonderful thing: whatever we do in his name, it is a continuation of Christ's own work, Christ the carpenter as much as the preacher.

The Holy Spirit is the vital essence of a live faith. He is the major secret in every Christian endeavor, not an extra or a bonus for those who can be bothered and are interested, but the guarantee, the gift. The Church has often treated him as a sort of quest, a Holy Grail or reward for those who try extra hard. We are weak and imperfect and that is why Christ sent the Spirit; he makes the feeble effective. If we feel we are wanting, the answer is to want the Holy Spirit! Without the Spirit we have only ideas, advice and ethics. With the Spirit we have a dynamic not a dead doctrine.

The Spirit waits for the Word

A very important and special thing to note is that the Spirit follows the word. The word of God and the Holy Spirit are linked many times, but always in a dynamic relationship. Here are some typical passages:

"All Scripture is God-breathed" (2 Timothy 3:16). The Spirit and the word work together. "Breath" is Spirit, the breath of God. He breathes the word of God.

"The Spirit of God was hovering over the waters. And God said, 'Let there be light' and there was light" (Genesis 1:2-3).

"Moses stretched out his hand over the sea and all that night the Lord drove the sea back with a strong east wind. Moses and the Israelites sang, 'By the blast of your nostrils the waters piled up. You blew with your breath, and the sea covered the enemy. They sank like lead in the mighty waters'" (Exodus 14:21, 15:1, 8-10).

"Then he said to me, 'Prophesy to the breath; prophesy, son of man, and say to it, This is what the Sovereign Lord says: Come from the four winds, O breath, and breathe into these slain, that they might live'" (Ezekiel 37:9).

"Prophecy never had its origin in the will of man, but men spoke from God as they were carried along by the Holy Spirit" (2 Peter 1:21).

In each quotation the Spirit of God works with the spoken word. The principle is an important truth: the Spirit moves when the word is spoken, never spontaneously at his own will. He only fulfils the will of God expressed by the word of God, whoever speaks it. He acts in accordance with the word of God whether we speak it or God.

At Creation the Holy Spirit hovered over the dark waters. He is the creative Spirit, but he did nothing. When God spoke, the word came and he changed the chaos to beauty and order. Again, when the prophets presented the word of God, the Holy Spirit inspired them. In Acts 2:4 we are told that the 120 disciples began to speak in tongues, declared the mighty acts of God as the Spirit enabled them.

The Spirit and the word are interlocked, inseparable. *"When the Counselor comes, whom I will send to you from the Father, he will testify about me. He will bring glory to me by taking from what is mine, and making it known to you"* (John 15:26, 16:14). Jesus said, *"The Son can do nothing by himself; he can only do what he sees the Father doing. Even so the Son gives life to whom he is pleased to give it"* (John 5:19,21).

The supreme example is the Holy Spirit working with the Living Word, Jesus. The Holy Spirit is committed irretrievably to the word and inseparable from the word. He is not an unattached power; he is *"the Spirit of truth."* He is the truth behind the word of God as we read the Scriptures.

The Spirit is permanently committed to the word but not to our own human word, however brilliant, humorous or interesting it might be – unless we speak according to the truth of the word. *"To the law and to the testimony! if they do not speak according to this word, they have no light of dawn"* (Isaiah 8:20).

The Holy Spirit was absent from the world and did not work until *"the Word became flesh and made his dwelling among us"* (John 1:14). Certain chosen men and women had known his fleeting help only, for specific tasks. Then Jesus, the Living Word, came and the Holy Spirit was with him. The Spirit waited for the Word to appear before the world. John the Baptist said that when Jesus was baptized in the Jordan River, *"I saw the Spirit come down from heaven as a dove and remain on him"* (John 1:32).

The Spirit awaited the coming of the Word and then the word of the Spirit came. That is the normal pattern of things. In 1 Peter 1:12 we read that things were told *"by those who have preached the gospel to you by the Holy Spirit sent from heaven."* It is not much good any other way. It is useless preaching about the Spirit without the Spirit. It was never intended to be like that. Jesus would not let the disciples go out with the gospel until the Spirit came.

People wonder at the early church. The first Christian converts were not sophisticated in Christian ways at all. Separation for them meant from sexual sins, dishonesty, and thieving. The kind of instructions that Peter and Paul needed to send to churches in those days would offend respectable church members today. John Wesley told his preachers to keep free of lice, a social scourge in those days, but the lives of Corinthian converts called for rather different exhortations. Yet God by his Spirit made the word mighty in that city.

If we wait until we are fully satisfied with ourselves, our habits and sanctification, we would never start witnessing at all. In any case, if we fancy that we are advanced in spirituality, that would be conceit and hardly the attitude the Holy Spirit would anoint.

This fact should encourage us – the gospel is the catalyst for the power of God. Preach the word and it releases the Spirit. Perfection is in the word, not in us. The word is the key, the seed, and the secret. If we want the Spirit in our lives, we have to begin with the word. The baptism in the Spirit experience springs from conviction of the word. To seek the Holy Spirit and neglect the word of God is to seek power without purpose, merely for personal gratification. Is that what anybody really wants?

The message of Christ is critical for mankind. It is always the red alert. God is not likely to withhold help for any reason where help is needed. Many talk about revival and invent a hundred reasons why it is slow in coming. Is God like that? What kind of God would let people slide down to perdition unhindered because he saw flaws in church members? Is the Holy Spirit likely to be put off by our incomplete spiritual education when the whole world needs to be saved?

Jesus sends us. C. T. Studd, who pioneered missionary work in Africa with absolute dedication 70 years ago, said that we do not need any mandate to go other than the word of God. To go, that is the way to perfection. There can be none without it. Follow Jesus. Go where he went, full of love and concern for the people. As you go you will learn from him and about him, what he is. Getting to know him better as you go is the true way to cultivate your soul.

How the Holy Spirit works

The first verses of Scripture tell us things about the Spirit that are seen all the way through the Bible.

"In the beginning God created the heavens and the earth. Now the earth was formless and empty, darkness was over the surface of the deep and the Spirit of God was hovering over the waters. And God said, 'Let there be light' and there was light" (Genesis 1:1-3).

Here are the main points in that text:

1. God created heaven and earth.
2. The earth was shapeless, empty, dark and lifeless.
3. The Spirit of God was present, hovering over the waters.
4. God spoke and the Spirit of God went into action.

The earth was desolate and the Spirit of God was hovering there but he did nothing. We are not told how long the Spirit of God waited. Eventually God spoke: *"God said, 'Let there be light!'"* The Spirit went into action and *"there was light."*

The Holy Spirit did nothing until God spoke. The Spirit did not put on a solo act, functioning independently. He waited for the word. *"In the beginning was the Word. Without him nothing was made that has been made"* (John 1:1-3). Where Genesis says that God spoke, John tells us that it was the Word. The Living Word called out and the Holy Spirit did the Father's will.

"By the word of the Lord were the heavens made, the starry host by the breath of his mouth. He spoke, and it came to be; he commanded, and it stood firm" (Psalm 33:6,9). *"In the beginning was the Word. Through him all things were made"* (John 1:1,3). *"By God's word the heavens existed and the earth was formed"* (2 Peter 3:5). *"His Son ... through whom he made the universe, sustaining all things by his powerful word. By faith we understand that the universe was formed at God's command"* (Hebrew 1:2-3, 11:3).

The Holy Spirit always responds to the word. The word is never without the Spirit and the Spirit does not operate without the word. In Revelation John was told by Christ to write. He wrote 7 letters to 7 churches and each letter contains these words: *"He who has an ear, let him hear what the Spirit says to the churches."* The Holy Spirit said what Christ told John to write. It is a permanent partnership. *"And now the Sovereign Lord has sent me, with his Spirit"* (Isaiah 48:16). *"My word that goes out from my mouth will not return to me empty but will accomplish what I desire and achieve the purpose for which I sent it"* (Isaiah 55:11).

Not only Creation, but all of God's activities are initiated by the word. The whole of Psalm 29 celebrates the power and majesty of the Lord with ten actions by his word. *"He sent forth his word and healed them"* (Psalm 107:20).

In the beginning the Spirit of God worked by the Living Word, and today he works by the written word. Psalm 119:50 (NKJV) says, *"Your word has given me life."* In that Psalm the word is the law, testimonies, statutes, and precepts. The Spirit responding to the word renders the word effective, a fountain of life. Scripture is the conduit, the pipeline for the Holy Spirit. That is where we go to enjoy what God is, says and does, the Holy Spirit's channel for renewal, distinct from every other book.

The Holy Spirit partnered the Living Word and now partners the written word. The business of the Spirit is strictly the word of God. He does not listen to other voices. When Christ came, he was the Word, and the Holy Spirit worked as he spoke. Jesus applied Isaiah 61:1 to himself: *"The Spirit of the Sovereign Lord is on me."* Jesus spoke about his words, saying, *"The words I have spoken to you are spirit and they are life. Whoever hears my word and believes him who sent me has everlasting life"* (John 6:63, 5:24). The word was meant to be our business also. Our business secret is the Holy Spirit.

The word of God is a body of living truth. The bloodstream of Christ runs through the Book and God has breathed life into it. The Bible is here with us because it lives, and living things do not need preserving. The church has not preserved the Bible; the Bible has preserved the church. It is not an ancient document, a fossil; it speaks with a voice for today. It is the only book of power and joy by which we can live. It is oxygen for the soul, an atmosphere in which we can live. The church is not a society for the preservation of saint's bones. It is the church of the living God, the pillar and ground of the truth.

Revival

"Revival" comes about by the Holy Spirit responding to the preached word. The Holy Spirit does nothing without the word. All extraordinary events chosen to be called revivals and every real advance of the Christian faith came about through the word being preached. That is the pattern depicted in the New Testament.

"Man does not live on bread alone, but on every word that comes from the mouth of God" (Matthew 4:4). Love the word, live on it, with it, in it and by it, if we do that, we live a "live" life. Without it we are spiritually anorexic. Many cut down their intake, starve themselves or live with only bits, scraps and odd crumbs, no solid meat, not even the milk of the word. They are wilderness Christians. They exist on daily readings, manna sent them day by day while God's wish is for them to enjoy the fruits of the Land of Promise. Israel grumbled about the manna that they were given: *"We detest this miserable food"* (Numbers 21:5). If the Bible has been replaced by the Promise Box or the tear-off calendar, then to get an appetite for the word, simply read it!

We need to realize that without the word the Spirit will do little. By contrast, we can be what we should be, fulfill our potential, by the word. *"His divine power has given us everything we need for life and godliness, his very great and precious promises"* (2 Peter 1:3-4). *"All Scripture is God-breathed so that the man of God may be thoroughly equipped for every good work"* (2 Timothy 3:16-17). *"Let the word of Christ dwell in you richly as you sing psalms"* (Colossians 3:16).

We are commanded to be full of the Spirit and that means being full of the word! You cannot have one without the other. Jesus said, *"I have told you this so that my joy may be in you. If my words remain in you, ask whatever you wish and it will be given you"* (John 15:11,7). Colossians 3:16 instructs us to *"sing psalms, hymns and spiritual songs"* as we *"let the word of Christ dwell in us richly."* Do our songs draw inspiration from the word of Christ and teach us?

The Holy Spirit is not commissioned to anoint our own ideas. People constantly pray, "Bless me, O Lord!" Often there it too much "me" and little "engrafted word." He will bless us if his word is in us. Jesus said, *"Blessed are those who hear the word of God and obey it"* (Luke 11:28). Jeremiah 17:8 says, *"Blessed is the man who trusts in the Lord, whose confidence is in him. He will be like a tree planted by the water that sends out its roots by the stream. It does not fear when heat comes; its leaves are always green. It has no worries in a year of drought and never fails to bear fruit."* The first Psalm also describes a godly man as being like a tree on the riverbank and shows what it is to trust in the Lord: *"Blessed is the man whose delight is in the law of the Lord and on his law he meditates day and night"* (Psalm 1:1-2).

The Scriptures are God-breathed (2 Timothy 3:16) – by the Spirit. The Bible is like a flowering garden, each page a seed plot of beauty. The sun shines on a garden and the flowers open to its warmth, absorb its rays and grow by it, by the process of photosynthesis, breathing in and then breathing out. They exhale perfume making the air fragrant. As Mary's alabaster box of ointment filled the house with fragrance, this is what happens when we break open the word. Its beauty is pervasive.

The Spirit and the Word at Work

From the moment the disciples received the Spirit, he activated the word of God. *"They preached the gospel by the Holy Spirit sent from heaven"* (1 Peter 1:12). That was never known before. The great Hebrew prophets never won any converts. Ezekiel said that God would *"make things a ruin"* (Ezekiel 21:27). Jeremiah ended his ministry lamenting over the smoldering ruins of Jerusalem, his word fulfilled. Jesus said that he would send the Spirit and that he would convict the world of sin, righteousness and judgment. Peter's first sermon brought 3,000 people to repentance.

John the Baptist, the greatest of the prophets, *"never performed a miraculous sign"* (John 10:41). He was the last of the old order but even the least in the kingdom is greater because they belong to a new age of the Spirit. The Spirit is the Lord of wonders. He is at work when we provide the channel, and that channel is the word as we preach it and live it and believe it. *"He will speak only what he hears"* (John 16:13). What things does he hear, when and where?

He hears the word, nothing else. When he hears it, he speaks and drives it home. He hears it when we speak it. The Spirit shows Jesus to be what the word says about him.

The Holy Spirit is the Spirit of Christ: *"The Spirit of Christ who was in them"* (1 Peter 1:11), *"the Spirit of Jesus"* (Acts 16:7), *"The Spirit of Jesus Christ"* (Philippians 1:19). Christ's Spirit naturally belongs to Christ, the Word, and works with him. Jesus declared, *"I will send to you from the Father the Spirit of truth. Unless I go away, the Counselor will not come to you; but if I go, I will send him to you"* (John 15:26, 16:7). He also said, *"He will bring glory to me by taking from what is mine and making it known to you"* (John 16:14). The Spirit is to be to us what Jesus was to the disciples.

Jesus alone gives the Spirit. He alone baptizes in the Holy Spirit. Nobody else has any authority to bestow the Spirit. We can lay on hands but the Spirit comes from Christ. We receive the Spirit for ourselves with no surplus for us to give away. As John wrote, *"Of his fullness we have all received"* (John 1:16 NKJV) – not out of somebody else's fullness. There is no sharing the anointing.

Preaching the word brings the supply of the Spirit. Philippians 1:18-19 speaks of Christ being preached and that *"this will turn out for my deliverance ... through the supply of the Spirit of Jesus Christ."* The gospel is the power of God.

Recently Los Angeles had power cuts. The plants were not generating enough to meet the demand. Science informs us that the material universe is composed of energy. Einstein's famous equation is that mass equals energy. Every atom is a power pack. The problem of industry it to tap nature's infinite resources or energy. The sun is a power plant. Science knows how it works, knows the formula but has not yet been able to duplicate it. The problems are immense. It could solve the power needs of the whole world and fossil fuels would no longer be burned, polluting the atmosphere.

Are some churches like that? Using artificial power instead of Holy Spirit power? *"Every good and perfect gift is from above, coming down from the Father of the heavenly lights"* (James 1:17). God's infinite resources are available to us. Plenty of people quote Christ's words *"All power is given unto me in heaven and in earth"* (Matthew 28:18 KJV) and speak of God's omnipotence but seem to be suffering from a power cut. Paul wrote, *"I pray that the eyes of your heart may be enlightened in order that you may know his incomparably great power for us who believe. That power is like the working of his mighty strength, which he exerted in Christ when he raised him from the dead"* (Ephesians 1:18-20).

> The Holy Spirit always responds to the word. The word is never without the Spirit and the Spirit does not operate without the word.

Some believers think that the greatness of the power that Paul talks about was only for apostolic times. They even import ideas, theories and dispensations into Scripture that are quite simply never mentioned there. They are theories of unbelief, telling us that miracle times belong to the past, making parts of the New Testament irrelevant and Christianity different to when it began. Some think miracles then were more real than now, as if the Holy Spirit had come but was a force that diminished over time. The truth is that the power lines are not dead. If we believe, we will see the glory of God. Critics complain that evangelists build up hopes of miracles. No, they do not – the Bible does!

Others assume that they have to generate power by their own efforts, cranking the handle to generate a bit of current. They measure power by the amount of time they spend in prayer, by their degree of holiness or by the extent of their spiritual effort. They confuse human input with divine output.

The power stations of the cross and the resurrection have never shut down. Jesus is just as alive, the word of God is just as true as 2,000 years ago. Truth is timeless: *"His truth endures to all generations"* (Psalm 100:5). The Holy Spirit's energies, the power of the blood of Christ, the throbbing life of the Resurrection, the revelation of Christ at the right hand of God, these add up to a power message about a power experience.

God's power is as a great and needed by us now every bit as much as it was by the apostles. They were up against a cynical and un-believing world – and so are we; they did not let the world trouble them – and nor do we. The world was empty of hope, bankrupt of resources, with nothing at the end of life but a coffin. By contrast, the believers were clothed with strength, their minds lit by hope, their lives alive with regenerating forces. Hallelujah!

There is, however, a very simple fact: However high the voltage, if we do not plug in, do not switch on, no power comes through. We need what the apostles needed and shall get it if we do what the apostle did. Every home has a power point. Where is our power point? It is the word of God. Plug in – read and believe!

The Spirit and the Word are the two hands of the Father doing the Father's will. We read about God's right hand but never about a left hand. Why is that? Our left hand is usually weaker, less effi-cient than our right hand. God has no feeble left hand. There is no inefficiency in him. The Psalmist said, *"You have a mighty arm"* (Psalm 89:13). Christ is at God's right hand. It means that he **is** God's right hand. He wields all power. He is the Word and it is by him that the Holy Spirit performs wonders.

God never shows weakness, has no weak spot, and is never under par, off-hand, incidental or casual. God's power is not variable. We cannot put our foot on the throttle for an increase of God's power. It is not greater in one meeting than in another. Jesus did not say, "Where two or three are gathered together there I am, to some degree, depending on the atmosphere." There is only one power setting: *"I the Lord do not change"* (Malachi 3:6). He never takes on more than he can handle and never keeps something in reserve for when we deserve it. Our common expressions about "having more of God" or "more power" are not in the Bible. Any changes in spiritual temperature are in us, not in God.

We are instructed not to quench the Spirit. The Holy Spirit is quenched when we preach without the Spirit or without the word: *"The letter kills, but the Spirit gives life"* (2 Corinthians 3:6). Without the Spirit, preaching is lecturing, giving information that leaves the spiritual life of the church to wither. Some preachers talk like doctors to sick patients instead of fanning the flames of fervency. Of course, physical exertion and shouting do not generate the Holy Spirit, but then nor does being cool and precise. The Lord does not mind peculiarities of expression if they express his joy, but he is not interested in simulated effects. He shies away from slick preaching, manipulative psychology and egotistical tricks, rabble-rousing. The Spirit comes with the word. Every page blooms with fifty sermons. Why scrape the bottom of the barrel for sermons? *"Preach the word"* – it is a bottomless well.

A sermon starts with a man opening the Bible and having an experience with the Spirit. If the Bible is open to you, a sermon is your experience with God. That is unction, the anointing, an experience denied angels but so wonderful that perhaps it should be permitted only to angels, the greatest pleasure known. It is the same with witnessing. It is fulfilling and satisfying.

Questions

1. Why did the Church neglect the Holy Spirit for so long?
2. The Spirit waits for the word.
   Can you think of 3 examples?
3. What is the greatest example of the Spirit and the word?

"Then the end will come."
Matthew 24:14

The material world is not a temporary arrangement. When the present earth is finished there will be a new one. Human beings are special creatures, flesh and spirit, and will continue to be so in the resurrection. Just as Jesus continues to be the Son of Man. Creation is God's glory, for ever.

Jesus, the Son of God, will return to this world as the Son of Man (Mark 13:26, Matthew 24:37). When Jesus left this earth bodily, angels told the disciples that *"this same Jesus, who has been taken from you into heaven, will come back in the same way you have seen him go into heaven"* (Acts 1:11). Our Lord is part of the physical and material creation – his own creation.

His first coming was the incarnation, God in the flesh. It tells us that God's material order has full significance: God deals with us as human beings, not just spiritual beings. The world saw Christ working out our salvation visibly, in real physical labors, with prayer, shedding real blood on a real cross, and it was a real Jesus who broke out of the tomb of death. The earth is not foreign to God. He is as much at home here as in heaven. *"The earth is the Lord's, and everything in it"* (1 Corinthians 10:26).

This book has demonstrated that the gospel is for body and soul, physical as well as spiritual. The world is made in such a way that spiritual forces can operate in it. Miracles are possible because God planned for them in his creation. The world is constructed as a place where prayer is heard, and prayer was part of his plan for the proper running of a good world. If men never pray, then they are out of step with the way things are. The world is built on order, but it is God's order. We ourselves have the power to change things in nature without creating disorder, and so can God. Prayer moves the hand that moves the world. That is the way things were made.

Christ is returning to this world because he was born here, breathed and ate here, and his dying blood stained the earth. Earth is the home of the Son of Man, and he is at home here wherever people love him. *"If anyone loves me, my Father will love him, and we will come to him and make our home with him"* (John 14:23).

It is impossible to preach a gospel which is only good news about going to heaven and then talk about Jesus coming back and reigning on earth. When the Pentecostals began, they brought a revolution in Bible understanding. The talk had always been spiritual, especially "grace," a mystical influence. Grace at work produced spiritual effects only. The strange episodes of "revival" were the secret effect of grace, and when anyone turned to God, grace did it. But Pentecostals spoke of the Holy Spirit, and the Spirit has always been known to us as the third Person of the Godhead assigned to work on earth, even supernaturally. Jesus also worked in the spiritual and physical dimensions of life on earth and when he left, the Holy Spirit took his place.

Satan would like to send us to sleep waiting for the Bridegroom. Even in Peter's lifetime people were asking, *"Where is the 'coming' he promised?"* (2 Peter 3:4). Peter reminded them that time means nothing to God, for a thousand years is only like a day to him. Jesus will come when the Father decides. He is not tied down to a program of events. His coming is not at the end of a long road of signs, for the kingdom of God runs alongside us, and he can step over into our history at any time.

Jesus warned us that confusion and false teachers would appear before he came back – false prophets and false Messiahs. The glorious truth of Christ's return has been mishandled by people prophesying, calculating, predicting, and describing horrendous events that lie ahead. Dates have been fixed for his return, and when they have been wrong, new dates were simply fixed. The mysterious symbols of Revelation have spawned a thousand fantasy interpretations. Many have set themselves up as prophets using the prophecies of Scripture. Religious movements have been based on predictions of Christ's Second Advent, but their basis has been speculation, though such organizations engineer to survive their vital errors.

The world is due for a shock. At present it ignores the works of the Holy Spirit. The media find space in their columns and broadcasts for every kind of triviality and short-lived show. A murder will occupy time and attention, but what God is doing is not given a moment's thought. The Bible is muzzled as if it were a dangerous book (as indeed it is for unbelievers who read it). As Jesus said, *"As it was in the days of Noah, so it will be at the coming of the Son of Man. They knew nothing about what would happen until the flood came and took them all away"* (Matthew 24:37-39). People are willingly ignorant and his coming will come on them unawares.

As we explained in a previous chapter, when Jesus comes again, he will come with his hands raised in blessing. The suggestion that his coming will destroy those who are not saved is not what Scripture says. He came the first time not to destroy men's lives but to save them: *"God did not send his Son into the world to condemn the world but to save the world through him"* (John 3:17).

If he is to reign as King of kings, who will he reign over if everyone is condemned and dies? His coming is to bless the nations and turn them back to God. If he is to bring peace, who will he bring peace to except the peoples of the countries around the globe? Isaac Watts wrote rightly:

> *Blessings abound wher'er he reigns;*
> *The prisoner leaps to loose his chains,*
> *The weary find eternal rest*
> *And all the sons of want are blest.*

That is indeed the promise of the coming Jesus. I say "indeed" because Jesus Christ is the same yesterday, today and for ever. He is the great Lover of us all. If anyone teaches that he is no longer the same, that he no longer heals, no longer baptizes in the Spirit, no longer gives gifts to men, then he is not the same any more, and he has not kept his promises, people cannot expect him to come with blessings to save mankind and we have no future. However, we have every hope in him, in his compassionate care for us all. He is the God of hope.

The Pentecostal-charismatic revival movement has prepared us for the Jesus who is coming. We know what kind of king he is, for by his Spirit, his coming is already foreshadowed in works of mercy and power. That is the Jesus we look for and the Jesus who will not delay his return a single moment longer than he needs. He says he will come quickly and that is how it will be.

Nevertheless, nobody will get away with it. In his parables of the kingdom in Matthew 13, he tells us that the angels will go through his kingdom and remove the wicked and crush every institution of evil and injustice. If people hear the gospel and oppose it, or play fast and loose with God, the words of Jesus give them no comfort for their future. Where the gospel is preached every week and people pass by with a toss of the head, there is greater condemnation. They have light but walk in darkness and darkness is reserved for them when Christ comes.

The second coming of Christ is a vital basis for evangelism. When the first preachers went out, it was crucial to their message. Peter preached it in the first-ever gospel address and Paul preached it to the Athenian intellectuals. The apostle spent three weeks preaching to the Thessalonians but from the letter he subsequently sent them, we see that the return of Christ was a major element in his message. The last message in the Bible, which knits it all together into a dynamic whole, is *"I am coming soon"* (Revelation 22:20).

If we are to preach the word, there are scores of verses on Christ's coming that we can use. It is part of the good news. Preach the word, in season and out of season, and by all possible means save some!

The aim of every chapter in this third book of mine on evangelism is to provide instruction on as many angles of gospel truth as possible, to equip the man of God with tools, to put a rounded, informed message in his mouth, and to inspire vigor and faith. No one man can save the world, but at the beginning of the 21st century the Christian church is expanding rapidly, with every 10th person on earth already a believer; the evangelism of the whole world is feasible. So to the work – our goal is in sight! Be filled with the Spirit, fear nobody, and God will be with you.

No one man can save the world, but at the beginning of the 21st century the Christian church is expanding rapidly, with every 10th person on earth already a believer; the evangelism of the whole world is feasible. So to the work – our goal is in sight! Be filled with the Spirit, fear nobody, and God will be with you.

Give me, my Lord Jesus, a sense of the great privilege and joy of sharing with you in the works of the Father, by the Holy Spirit. Give me your word in its living form that I may represent it in my life to light up this dark world. I want to be what you want me to be. I know that we believers are your sole but chosen means by which you work your wonders. Amen!

Blessed are those who do not walk in step with the wicked
or stand in the way that sinners take
or sit in the company of mockers,
but who delight in the law of the Lord
and meditate on his law day and night.
They are like a tree planted by streams of water,
which yields its fruit in season and whose leaf does not wither
– whatever they do prospers.

Psalm 1:1-3

In evangelism there is no "right" way of doing things, only right principles, principles that can be drawn from the New Testament. The apostle Paul himself said, *"That I might by all means save some."* The test of what is "right" is whether the Holy Spirit makes it his chariot.

It is unfortunate that certain methods seem to become sacrosanct. We can fight with one another over traditions which may actually be non-functional; the machine itself becomes more greatly admired than the product. Being faithful and being a stick-in-the-mud are not the same thing. Christian faithfulness means being faithful to Christ's message. Circumstances may call for a new or radical approach but the fundamental objective is to reach people everywhere with the message of salvation and to touch them with the finger of Christ's love.

I am amazed by the brilliance of thought in the world church to-day. At the same time, brilliance may be an intellectual exercise on the periphery of life as opposed to hard work in the harvest field. Sadly, so much mental effort goes into doctrinal quibbles, technical irrelevancies and exercises in philosophical debate. If we are to go all out to "save some", it is, of course, legitimate to think about how we are going to do it. Genius is welcome and has a worthy subject in the gospel. The problem is if it stops there.

There are 32 chapters in this two-volume work. It was originally planned as a single volume but the material quickly became enough for two because there are so many matters vitally linked to the proclamation of the gospel of Christ. That is what I have learned in more than 30 years of devotion to the single purpose of bringing men and women into the Kingdom of God. Doing the work can be far more satisfying if we understand what we are really doing – measuring our activities against the standards set by the Word itself. Knowing the Word in the way taught in these chapters also means great efficiency. Psalm 1 promises *"whatever he does prospers"*. Who is the psalmist talking about? The previous verses have already identified him – the man who meditates on the Word …

Read more in Part II of

HELL EMPTY – HEAVEN FULL
Fulfilling the Mission

Notes

Learn how to be an explosive soul-winner!

Get ignited and have a fire kindling your evangelistic skills with 8 easy online lessons. Through Reinhard Bonnke's proven soul-winning experience and tools for evangelism, you will gain valuable insights and learn how to bring the world's lost to Christ.

Here's what the **School of Fire** will teach you:

- The basic principles of imparting the truth about the Fire
- The truth about Salvation
- Evangelism as explained in the Bible
- How to practice global Evangelism
- How to depend on the Holy Spirit
- Proven methods for Discipleship and Follow-up

The **School of Fire** will stir a passion for lost souls in you!

Study at your own pace while our comprehensive testing ensures that you have the skills you need to be an explosive soul-winner!

Register online today at:

www.schooloffire.com

and learn how to spread the fire!

FULL FLAME™
F I L M   S E R I E S

GNITING A PASSION FOR THE LOST

NEW!

An 8 part film series combines modern day and biblical stories with the teachings of Reinhard Bonnke in a sweeping cinematic presentation on soul-winning.

Empower your church today with a Master Pack, complete with discussion guides, 8 DVDs, an inspirational music CD, and principles on revolutionary evangelism.

***Join the battle cry for the heart of mankind.
Be ignited to share your faith.***

CfaN
CHRIST
FOR ALL NATIONS

INTEGRITY
MEDIA™

For more information,
www.fullflamemovie.com

Evangelism by Fire

Igniting Your Passion for the Lost

Evangelism by Fire will give you an insight into the God-inspired anointing of Reinhard Bonnke. This book will fire your faith and give you the encouragement to believe God for the impossible. Evangelism by Fire is a powerful and practical presentation of the principles which the Lord has taught him over the years.

320 pages • ISBN 3-935057-19-9

Audiobook
10 CDs • ISBN 0-9758789-2-1

Workbook
88 pages • ISBN 3-935057-28-8

Time is running out

There are more lost souls than ever – and less time than ever to save them. Now the evangelist's evangelist calls us – and helps us – to redouble our efforts to win over the world for Jesus. Reinhard Bonnke's unbridled passion for winning souls dates back to his youth. He is acclaimed worldwide for a ministry that has one avowed, all-consuming purpose – plunder hell to populate heaven! Poignant, exhorting and uncompromising, this dramatic book combines the author's excitement for evangelism with his proven, effective techniques for reaching the lost of this world. It is a resounding call for each of us to reexamine our priorities, heed the call of Christ, preach the good news, and save people from hell.

252 pages • ISBN 3-935057-60-1

Workbook
88 pages • ISBN 3-935057-85-7

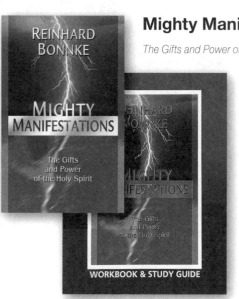

Mighty Manifestations

The Gifts and Power of the Holy Spirit

This book gives us a 'back to the Bible' examination of the spiritual gifts listed in 1 Corinthians 12. These are not given so that we may congratulate ourselves, or polish up our church's images, but to endorse the preaching of the Gospel to those around us. This is a book not only to increase our understanding, but to energise us for action.

298 pages • ISBN 3-935057-00-8

Workbook
72 pages • ISBN 3-935057-27-X

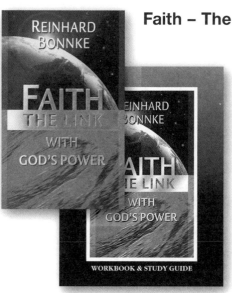

Faith – The Link with God's Power

Some believe that simply having faith is an entitlement to blessing and prosperity. Others believe that faith in oneself is all that is needed in life. Still others contend that faith is a cosmic force that breeds superhuman, super-spiritual, invincible people. In this book, Reinhard Bonnke reveals the truth about faith towards God, drawing from his many years of personal study and experience.

292 pages • ISBN 3-935057-29-6

Workbook
72 pages • ISBN 3-935057-26-1

*All text books are accompanied by **workbooks** as study guide – for your personal use, Sunday school or study groups. They will enable you to work out the truth and practical applications of having a vital and dynamic faith for yourself, as well as gaining deeper insights into the work and ministry of the Holy Spirit in relation to your personal life. These workbooks are a must for each reader of the text book!*

Even Greater

On one level, these dramatic stories are a testimony to the life and work of Reinhard Bonnke. The awesome numbers of souls eternally changed by the Cross of Jesus Christ through Bonnke's preaching are incredible by any human standard. Yet Reinhard is quick to give credit where credit is due – from "zero to hero" he often says, referring to God's grace poured into his life and ministry. This theme of empowering grace pushes each story to a higher level.

Everyone has a dream, or perhaps had a dream. These are stories of real people, Reinhard included, who through failure, weakness, and just bad circumstances watched their dreams evaporate. But God was not finished. He had even greater plans prepared for them, as He has even greater plans for you.

His grace is freely given!

You will be moved ... You will be inspired ... You will be challenged ...
to do even greater works for God.

ISBN 0-9758789-0-5 • 192 pages